DAVE EGGERS and VENDELA VIDA

Away We Go

Dave Eggers is the author of *What Is the What* and *Zeitoun*, among other books. He is the founder and editor of McSweeney's and the co-founder of 826 National, a network of tutoring and writing labs for youth. With Spike Jonze he cowrote the screenplay to *Where the Wild Things Are*, to be released in the Fall of 2009.

Vendela Vida is the author of books including *And Now You Can Go* and *Let the Northern Lights Erase Your Name*—both of which were *New York Times* Notable Books of the Year. She is a founding co-editor of *The Believer* magazine, and the editor of *The Believer Book of Writers Talking to Writers*. Her new novel, *The Lovers*, will be published in 2010.

Away We Go

A SCREENPLAY
WRITTEN BY

Dave Eggers and Vendela Vida

Vintage Books
A DIVISION OF RANDOM HOUSE, INC.
NEW YORK

FIRST VINTAGE BOOKS EDITION: JUNE 2009

Screenplay © 2009 Focus Features LLC.

All rights reserved. Published in the United States by Vintage Books, a division
of Random House, Inc., New York, and in Canada by Random House of
Canada Limited, Toronto.

Vintage and colophon are registered trademarks of Random House, Inc.

ISBN: 978-0-307-47588-6

Book design by R. Bull

www.vintagebooks.com

Printed in the United States of America
10   9   8   7   6   5   4   3   2   1

Dear Readers of Screenplays,

Welcome to the screenplay of *Away We Go*. We've attempted to make this readable to a non-screenwriting population, from whose ranks we recently came. That is, we were not really screenwriters when we made an attempt to tell this story; we undertook the task having no expectation that an actual movie would emerge from the process. That it has become a movie filmed by and filled with wildly talented people is beyond surreal.

We started this whole thing back in 2005. We were expecting our first child, and found ourselves sitting together a lot, listening to heartbeats and feeling for kickings, and reading pregnancy and birthing books—and laughing about the more ludicrous aspects of the pregnancy-birthing-childrearing-industrial complex. We started taking notes and making up characters, and then we started writing dialogue, and then a few scenes, and soon we were writing a full-blown screenplay on actual screenwriting software that we paid money for in a store.

Verona and Burt were written with Maya Rudolph and John Krasinski in mind, and we're still astonished that these two wonderfully humane and funny people gave flesh to these characters. When we conceived them, we thought of a couple who was as different from ourselves as we could muster. Burt and Verona are unmoored and unmarried, and Burt's parents, the impending baby's grandparents, are about to fly off to Belgium. Thankfully, we have no personal experience with Belgium-trotting grandparents, nor do we know any of the characters who Burt and Verona encounter on this trip. But we have been to Miami, so that part of the script—where we describe the South Beach promenade—is based on personal observation.

A few years after we wrote it, the script made its way to Sam Mendes, a British man who often wears scarves. He didn't seem to have any real experience directing anything, especially plays and movies, but we decided to take a chance, in the hope that perhaps the job would enable him to buy a razor.

Oh ha ha. That was a joke. Sam actually had directed plays and movies, though he was still considered British. When he said he'd be interested in directing the movie, we were very happy, and became happier everytime he improved the script with his notes and suggestions. In fact, he was so careful with the text we'd written, and so collaborative, and so smart and surgical in the betterments he asked of us, that we began asking him advice in all matters, financial and personal, and, most of all, those relating to parallel parking.

The actors, when given the script, improved the dialogue more. In case you did not know this first-hand, we have to convey to you this: actors really know what they're doing. They get very serious about the words on the page, and they embody them, and they think about the characters they're playing (more than you have), and then they say the words you've written and make them far, far better. Sitting down with Maya Rudolph and John Krasinski the first time, and hearing them say the words... There is nothing like that. Hearing Catherine O'Hara and Jeff Daniels riff on the script, ad-libbing the shit out of every scene and killing everyone on set—it was something to see.

The process, in the end, was dream-like and far more fun than should be allowed. And the resulting movie is far more than what we'd hoped for. As people who usually sit alone and write for years on end, it's insanely gratifying to see gifted professionals envision and improve upon all of your skeletal ideas. The production design was great. The cinematography was incredible. The music. The editing. The clothes even. We'd like to thank all of these people—Jess Goncher, Ellen Kuras, Alexi Murdoch and Randall Poster, Sarah Flack, John Dunn—and everyone else involved at every stage.

Sally Willcox, not only a wonderful person and agent but also the all-star, never-sleeping president of the board of 826LA, was the script's first reader and champion. She gave it to Ed Saxon, a producer of vast experience and a man unafraid to wear, even in the most formal situations, a tie-dyed shirt made by his six-year-old daughter. For their ocean-deep generosity and kindness we'd also like to thank Jonathan Dayton and Valerie Faris. For running a great and friendly and smart small studio we need to acknowledge James Schamus, John Lyons, and everyone else on the happy ship called Focus Features. And Big Beach, where that happy ship landed (did we just stretch that metaphor to the breaking point?) features two kind men named Mark Turtletaub and Peter Saraf, and we're grateful to them for unflagging support.

And mostly, endlessly, we'd like to thank Sam Mendes for being a good friend to the written word, and to us.

The following script of *Away We Go* closely resembles the movie as released in June 2009. You'll also find scenes that were cut, by mutual decision. Sam didn't cut anything we felt should remain in the movie. Every decision was made jointly, or at least agreed upon jointly. But we felt it would be good to include some of these deleted scenes, including the script's original, admittedly radical Bush-era ending, for your reading pleasure.

We'll leave you with that—our wish for your pleasure—and also this: for the aspiring screenwriters out there, try to find a director disinclined to removing and barbecuing your innards.

Vendela Vida and Dave Eggers
2009

Away We Go

DIRECTED BY
Sam Mendes

WRITTEN BY
Dave Eggers & Vendela Vida

CAST

BURT..John Krasinski
VERONA ....Maya Rudolph
GRACE ....Carmen Ejogo
GLORIA ....Catherine O'Hara
JERRY...Jeff Daniels
LILY..Allison Janney
LOWELL ....Jim Gaffigan
ASHLEY ....Samantha Pryor
TAYLOR ....Conor Carroll
LN ....Maggie Gyllenhaal
RODERICK ....Josh Hamilton
WOLFIE ....Bailey Harkins
BABY NEPTUNE ....Brendan and Jaden Spitz
TOM ....Chris Messina
MUNCH...Melanie Lynskey
JAMES ....Colton Parsons
KATYA ....Katherine Vaskevich
IBRAHIM ....Jerome Walter Stephens
CAMMIE ....Brianna Eunmi Kim
COURTNEY ....Paul Schneider
ANNABELLE ....Isabelle Moon Alexander
PROFESSOR RUBY......................................Finnerty Steeves
PERFORMANCE MOM ....Stephanie Kurtzuba
BECKETT...Pete Wiggins
GWEN ....Audrey Amey
DANA..Shirley Roeca
CARRIE ....Tory Wood
DANCER GUYS ....Michael Breckley, Steve Lai,
                                        Randy Lee, Duane Sequira
DANCER GIRLS ....Vivien Eng, Leah O'Donnell
VALET ....Hector Flores
STAR SPANGLED BANNER SINGER....Alexandra Henderson

INT. BURT AND VERONA'S HOUSE — BEDROOM — NIGHT

We are moving silently through a small house. We see fishing gear, snow-shoes, paintings of skeletons. It's a messy, ramshackle, but still somehow charming place.

We arrive in the bedroom, where we see a woman, about 30, lying in bed, her head propped up by four pillows. She's wearing a negligee. It's very dark—we see only her silhouette.

> VERONA

Burt?

Now we see that there's a man under the covers, busying himself with her nether regions.

> BURT
> *(from under the sheets)*

What?

> VERONA

Don't.

There's some shuffling from Burt.

> BURT

Why?

> VERONA

Come back up. I want to kiss you.

More shuffling in the bed.

                              BURT

          C'mon. I want to do this. I'm staying down
          here.

                             VERONA
                            (sighing)

          Okay.

Verona tries to enjoy herself.

                        VERONA *(cont'd)*
          Just don't blow.

                              BURT
          What?

                             VERONA
          Don't blow.

                              BURT
          Why would I blow?

                             VERONA
          I don't know why you do anything you do,
          Burt. Just don't blow.

                              BURT
                        (from underneath)
          Now stop moving. You're gonna love it.

                             VERONA
          Okay. No more talking.

Burt settles in for the task at hand, then pauses.

                                4

VERONA *(cont'd)*

What's wrong?

BURT

Nothing.

VERONA

Why'd you stop?

BURT
(thoughtful pause)
I'm trying to figure out the best way to say
what I'm about to say.

VERONA

Why do you have to say anything?

BURT

Rona, you taste different. You know that?

Verona sits up, sighing.

VERONA

No. How would I know that, Burt?
(trying to pull him up)
Get up here. I'm not talking to the top of
your head. You want me to shower?

Burt emerges from under the covers and stares at Verona.

BURT

No, you don't taste dirty, just different.
Kind of . . . fruity.
(something occurring to him)

5

You know, a woman can taste different depending on various cofactors.

Verona sits up.

> VERONA
> I don't want to hear this. And I thought we agreed you wouldn't use the word "cofactor."

> BURT
> I said I wouldn't misuse it. All I'm saying is that from what I've read about vaginal flavor—

> VERONA
> Jesus!

> BURT
> From what I've read, abrupt changes happen when a woman's either menopausal . . .
> *(registering a new, momentous thought)*
> Or . . .

Verona slugs him. He falls off the bed.

INT. BURT AND VERONA'S CAR—DRIVING—NIGHT

It's November, the remains of snow on the ground. Verona and Burt have just gone to the drugstore for pregnancy tests—they've bought three—and are driving home.

Verona's driving, with Burt in the passenger seat.

BURT FARLANDER *is 33, white, tall, looking like he could be either an assistant professor or a lunatic shooting people from a tower—there's that funny-crazy look in his eyes. He's very straightforward and earnest, but also eccentric—the type of guy who's never done drugs, but has often gone camping nude. He reads widely but not deeply enough, and has many strange hobbies, which he indulges for short periods of time but with utter seriousness. The last such hobby was bear-tracking. Like his father, he works in the insurance business.*

VERONA DE TESSANT *is 34 and of mixed race—her mom was white, her father black. Her parents were both academics who taught at the University of South Carolina. She's cute, funny, and has problem hair, which she's constantly trying to tame with various styles and accessories—braids, curls, pins, a scarf—though the results vary. Still, her beauty and sense of humor are alluring and inspire many admirers.*

She's a medical illustrator and has the necessary combination of the artistic and the exacting. Of the pair, she is the more socially presentable and stable, and finds herself apologizing for her partner at least once a week. Still, she is devoted to him and he to her.

> VERONA
>
> Nope. I can't wait.

> BURT
>
> What?

> VERONA
>
> I'm pulling over.

> BURT
>
> We're ten minutes away. No.

She pulls over.

> BURT *(cont'd)*
> What're you . . .

EXT. HIGHWAY SHOULDER — NIGHT

Verona is already out of the car and pushing down her jeans.

> BURT
> At least get off the shoulder!

Sounds of urine hitting gravel.

> BURT *(cont'd)*
> It'll be less accurate out here.

> VERONA
> What?

> BURT
> You're supposed to do this in a bathroom.
> The air out here is different. The
> alkaline . . .

> VERONA
> The alkaline? The alkaline? Just . . .
> please. I'm done. Hold this on the end
> here. Verona hands him the stick. He holds
> it at a distance, the way you would a steam-
> ing pot, while she pulls up her pants.

VERONA *(cont'd)*

Lay it flat.

BURT

Lay it flat? Like on the road? Should I lay it on the road?

VERONA

No . . . on the dashboard or something.

Verona gets back in the driver's seat.

INT. BURT AND VERONA'S CAR — NIGHT

They're in the car, staring at the stick, which has been placed on the dash.

VERONA

It's time. Turn on the light.

Burt turns on the light. It's far too dim to see anything.

VERONA *(cont'd)*

That's the light? That's your interior light?

BURT

What? Yes that's my interior light! What's wrong with my interior light? You've never had a problem with my interior light before . . .

VERONA

Just— Shut up. Turn on the headlights.

She gets out and slams the door.

EXT. HIGHWAY SHOULDER — IN FRONT OF THE CAR — NIGHT

They're crouched on the gravel of the shoulder, both bathed in the white light of the headlights.

> VERONA
>
> Damn. I can't tell. Go do a control sample. Here.

She hands him a second stick from the package.

> BURT
>
> No. This is insane. Let's do it in the bathroom.

Verona gives him a look. Burt turns away from the car. Sounds of urine hitting gravel.

> VERONA
>
> Okay, now bring it over here.

> BURT
>
> But you said not on the road.

> VERONA
>
> I don't care what I said. We need the light.

Verona lays Burt's stick next to the other one on the road. Her movements are meticulous, precise. Burt reads the instructions while they're waiting.

BURT
So basically, one line is nothing, two lines
is . . .

Verona holds up both test sticks to the beam of the headlight. It's an intimate moment, and the tone changes from madcap to ethereal. Verona looks at Burt, wide-eyed.

VERONA
Holy mother of God.

EXT. COLORADO TOWN — FIRST LIGHT OF DAWN

We see a quick montage of local landscapes—mountains, trees, valleys, snow-capped peaks, ex-urban sprawl. This is where our couple lives.

The montage blends seamlessly into a new, strange kind of landscape.

The sun is rising over a hill. It's beautiful but also stark and perhaps even eerie, given that the hill is caramel-colored.

INT. BURT AND VERONA'S BEDROOM — FIRST LIGHT OF DAWN — MONTHS LATER (MARCH)

We back up a few inches and realize that the camera has lined up so Verona's belly—five months pregnant—looks like a small round mountain, and the sun appears to be rising behind it. Burt appears in close up behind Verona's belly.

INT. BURT AND VERONA'S BEDROOM—
MORNING—LATER

We hear vague sounds of scraping.

Verona wakes up, turns over, sees Burt sitting up, with a knife and a piece of wood. The wood is about six inches long, and very sad-looking, like a wooden carrot.

> BURT
> Hey. I'm glad you're up.

> VERONA
> What are you doing?

> BURT
> What does it look like? I'm cobbling.

Verona laughs.

> BURT *(cont'd)*
> I want to be a dad who knows how to carve stuff out of wood. I want our kid to get up in the morning, put on her hip-waders, walk out to the back porch, and find me cobbling.

> VERONA
> You're not cobbling. And why would she be wearing hip-waders?

BURT
(*he briefly considers answering the second
question but realizes he can't, so moves
onto the first*)
I am cobbling. Look. I've got a knife and
this wood and I'm making a toy . . .
(*looking at the shapeless blob of wood*)
. . . stick. I'm cobbling.

VERONA
You're not. That's not what it's called.

BURT
Of course it is. How would you know? You
don't have one of these.
(*indicating the knife*)

VERONA
Burt, cobbling is shoes. That's why the
people who make shoes are called cobblers.
You're not cobbling. You're carving. Or
whittling.

*Burt thinks for a while. It dawns on him that she's right. This takes some
of the appeal out of it for Burt. He stops carving. He rests his pathetic
wooden worm/stick on Verona's stomach.*

BURT
Look, she likes it. I saw her kick.

VERONA
No you didn't.

BURT

I can do other things, too. I just bought a
book about knots. Three hundred knots,
and I'm gonna learn them all. And I'm
gonna build a kiln.

Verona goes into the bathroom.

VERONA

Remember we go to your parents' house
this afternoon.

Burt calls from the other room.

BURT (O.S.)

I was thinking—we really have to get some
bigger bats.

No response from Verona. He reenters the room and stands in the doorway.

BURT *(cont'd)*

I know the reasonable part of you agrees
with me.

VERONA

We're fine, Burt. You already set up your
whole apparatus.

Burt moves into the living room while getting dressed.

*Behind him, just inside the front door, Burt has set up a bat-holder, where
he keeps three bats for home protection—one standard aluminum bat, one
plain wooden bat, and one much-more-threatening wooden bat with three
nails driven through it.*

BURT

I need more weapons if something happens
to you two.

VERONA

What would happen to us?

BURT

Good. I knew you'd be with me on this.
I'm gonna price some crossbows on the way
home. I have that family defense class
today.

Burt emerges from the bedroom wearing camouflage pants and boots. He's clearly trying to look like a commando, but the jerry-rigged result is unconvincing.

VERONA

Does anyone else there dress like that?

Burt moves into the living room, looking for something in the cluttered living room.

BURT

Where are those goggles you had?

VERONA

My airbrush ones? You can't use them.

He finds them hanging from the lamp on Verona's drafting table and grabs them.

BURT

Thanks.

> (putting them on)
>
> I'll be back at three. Might be later if we get into some empty-hand offense. See you guys.

He leans down to kiss Verona's lips passionately and her stomach gently, and then walks out the door and down the hallway.

EXT. BURT AND VERONA'S HOUSE — MORNING

We follow Burt out the door, where we see that they live in a small ranch house, one step up from a trailer, attached to a small grungy yard. He gets into a crumbling old Volvo and drives off.

INT. BURT AND VERONA'S CAR — MORNING

Burt is driving and listening to a Teach Yourself Mandarin *tape. He enthusiastically repeats some phrases.*

> TAPE
> *(first in English, then in Mandarin)*
> Do you own a boat?

> BURT
> *(repeats the Mandarin version while continually scraping the frost from the inside of his windshield)*

> TAPE
> Are you happy with your current insurance carrier?
> *(then in Mandarin)*

BURT
(repeats the Mandarin version)

TAPE
What kind of boat do you own?

INT. HOUSE — VERONA'S OFFICE/ STUDIO — MIDMORNING

The sounds of huffing and puffing. We think for a second that Verona's exercising, or in labor. Then we see Verona reclining on a couch staring at the TV.

On the TV a prenatal exercise video is playing. On screen, there are three women doing supra-geeky aerobic routines. They look like they're direct from 1986, with headbands and leg-warmers and poofy hair. The decor is ridiculous—as if they're exercising in a Price Is Right *living room interior.*

Verona is talking on the phone.

VERONA
I wish you could see this, Grace.

INT. GRACE'S OFFICE — PHOENIX — MIDMORNING

We see Grace, Verona's sister, on the other end of the phone.

GRACE *is striking-looking: caramel-skinned, thin, curvy. She's immaculately dressed, projecting an air of sophistication and professionalism. She paces around her office at work—a resort in Phoenix, dramatic desert view—with a hands-free device attached to her ear.*

VERONA

You want to hear the rhyming couplets?

You'll get much more from your pelvic floor
When you pass on the bagel
And do one more kegel

GRACE
(*laughing*)

No!

VERONA

You like that? Jesus. Grace, tell me: Do I
have to be uncool for the rest of my life?

Verona uses a remote to mute the TV. She grunts while getting off the couch.

GRACE

What are you doing? You're talking to me
while you're exercising?

VERONA

No, just watching it. I've got this subdural
hematoma thing due Friday. Trying to finish it before we go out tonight.

Verona sits down at her drafting table, and we see that her studio is a cramped and messy place—full of illustration board, canvases, hundreds of markers and small paint containers. All over the walls are unsettling photos of people and animals mid-surgery. A skeleton hangs in the corner.

Verona takes a brush in her hand and resumes working while still on the phone. We see that Verona is working on an illustration of one step of a brain surgery. It's a craniotomy—a flap of skin has been peeled back and a portion of skull removed, revealing the subject's brain.

GRACE
(surprised)
Out? You two? Where?

VERONA
Dinner at Burt's parents.

GRACE
(gently mocking, given this constitutes a big night out for Burt and Verona)
Oooh!
(now sincerely)
They must be out of their minds excited.

VERONA
You know them. I think they're actually happy to be the only set of grandparents. To have the baby to themselves.

GRACE
Don't say that.
(wistful)
You're lucky to have them so close.

VERONA
I know, I know. Believe me, we're gonna lean pretty hard on them.

GRACE

You know I'd be there if I could. I hate that
I'll be so far away. I'll just have to come and
take her on her first big adventure.

VERONA

What? When?

GRACE

Right away. I'm going to take her to
Barcelona and show her where I lost my
virginity.

VERONA

She's a fetus, Grace.

GRACE

Who do you think she'll look like?

VERONA

I hope she doesn't have Burt's . . .

GRACE

Facial hair?

VERONA
(laughs)

Feet.

GRACE

Those square feet.

VERONA

Like seal flippers.

Laughing, Verona lets her brush drift a bit.

> VERONA *(cont'd)*
> Oh shit. I just gave this guy's brain a vulva.

INT. KARATE-TYPE STUDIO — DAY

Burt is now in a class with a dozen other men, lined up in neat rows. The instructor is a Navy SEAL–type, also wearing goggles. Behind him are inflatable models of a wife and two small children. The wife is wearing a halter top and the children both have (real) iPods attached to them.

> INSTRUCTOR
> Will you be there to defend your family?

> BURT
> *(in unison with the others)*
> I will!

> INSTRUCTOR
> Do you have the skills to prevent them from being taken from you, leaving you bereft and emasculated?

> BURT
> *(in unison with the others)*
> I do!

With that, the instructor steps over to Burt and gives him a roundhouse kick to the side of the head. Burt goes down. We see the instructor from Burt's perspective, hovering over him, the inflatable family in the background.

INSTRUCTOR

Not yet you don't.

(*walking away*)

And not in those pants.

INT./EXT. CAR — DRIVING TO BURT'S PARENTS' HOUSE — LATE AFTERNOON

Verona is driving. Burt is holding ice to his head.

BURT

So lame.

VERONA

What?

BURT

Forget it.

(*changing his mind*)

Wait. Tell me something. Do I look like I can't jump from a two-story building?

VERONA

Wha—

BURT

Just tell me that. Just . . . let's say you see me on the street, and you have to make a judgment: can that guy jump from a second-story building or not?

VERONA

Burt—

BURT

Please. I need this.

VERONA
(*seriously*)

Yes. I think you could do it.

BURT

Thank you! But that guy . . . I'm not
going back there. I don't want to be around
anyone who doesn't believe I can do something I know I can do.
(*brushing it off*)
Whatever. It doesn't matter.

VERONA
(*very seriously*)

Burt. You've never failed at anything you
wanted to do. You just don't always want
to do the
(*finding the word*)
standard things.

Burt brightens instantly.

They pass over a river. The landscape is wintry and spare.

BURT

I really want her to have an epic kind of
childhood. I want her to run along the
streams and to know how to work a canoe,
and to be able to entertain herself when
she's outside. I want her childhood to be
Huck Finny, you know?

VERONA

I had that.

Burt wants Verona to continue. She never talks about her childhood. But she drops it.

BURT

. . . Exactly.

Burt's cellphone rings.

BURT *(cont'd)*

Burt Farlander.
(*listens*)
Oh you old so-and-so! Sorry about your
Pacers, my friend. If you think Mike Dun-
leavy can carry more than a bucket of
water, I have some Florida swampland you
might be interested in!

Burt laughs uproariously. This entire time, he's been speaking in the voice of a '50s radio announcer. Actually, it sounds eerily like Casey Kasem, and it's obvious that this voice-change Burt uses for clients drives Verona around the bend.

BURT *(cont'd)*

Well thanks for calling back. I wanted to
talk to you about hurricane season. I
just . . . No, I know you're covered, but are
you covered-covered?

When it's clear the call will go on for a few minutes, Verona pulls the car over on the highway and gets out, shutting Burt/Casey Kasem inside.

EXT. ROADSIDE — LATE AFTERNOON

Verona walks until Burt is inaudible, stops, and looks out over the grey landscape.

Finally Burt steps out of the car in the distance.

> BURT
> (*finishing up*)
> Okay then. I will! I will! Ha ha. Yes. Yes. Oh please. You're too much. Okay now. Talk to you soon.

Burt hangs ups and walks over to Verona.

> BURT (*cont'd*)
> They expect that from me.

> VERONA
> They expect you to sound like Casey Kasem.

> BURT
> Listen, Rona, these guys are all in their fifties and sixties. We're dealing with millions of dollars in insurance futures. They don't want to be dealing with some thirty-three-year-old who didn't finish college.

Beat.

> VERONA
> So Casey Kasem finished college?

Beat.

BURT

Yes.

She looks at him, annoyed. He nuzzles into her.

BURT (cont'd)
(in Casey Kasem voice)

This next one goes out to a very special girl. The letter reads: "Dear Casey. My girl-friend's pregnant and frustrated. Can you play a song that will make her smile? Thanks. Signed, Burt Farlander."

VERONA

Your pregnant girlfriend's going to kill you.

Burt leans in and kisses her, and she relents, and finally seems to enjoy it.

VERONA (cont'd)

Now go away.

INT. CAR — DRIVING TO BURT'S PARENTS' HOUSE — LATE AFTERNOON

They're back in the car.

VERONA

Do you think your mom's gonna grope me this time?

BURT

She loves you. She wants to be you.

VERONA

You think your dad's gonna say I look glorious?

BURT

Not glorious.

VERONA

What's his new favorite?
                    (arriving at it)
Superb!
              (now in Jerry's voice)
Superb! Your slacks! Superb!

*They pull into the driveway. It's a very clean upper-middle-class home, a
bit on the overwrought side.*

BURT

It's better than the last word.

VERONA
(still in Jerry's voice)
Verona. You. Are. Wonder-rous.

*They're gathering the cake and wine they've brought. They get out of the
car.*

BURT

Look, the guy just dodged prostate cancer.
He appreciates things now.

VERONA

He appreciates adjectives.

They approach the door.

VERONA *(cont'd)*
(remembering something)
Oh, your mom wants the baby to call her
Glammie. She told me yesterday.

BURT
(tasting the word)
Glammie . . . What does that mean?

VERONA

Half Gloria, half Grandma.
(off Burt's look)
And the glamour part.

EXT. BURT'S PARENTS' HOME — EVENING

Gloria bursts out of the door.

GLORIA
(to Verona)
Oh! Look at you! You look so big. Good for
you!

We see GLORIA—*about 54, very fit, in a denim jacket with a faux-fur
collar, turned up. Her hair is piled high in a vaguely Barbarella style,
though less intentional-seeming.*

BURT

Your hair. What'd you do?

GLORIA

I freed it!

BURT

I don't think it makes you look crazy at all.

GLORIA

I know! I know! Come in, your dad's finishing a call.

We hear Jerry in the distance, talking in the same Casey Kasem-like voice that Burt uses.

INT. BURT'S PARENTS' HALLWAY — EVENING

JERRY (O.S.)

Bill, if you believe that, I've got a bridge in New York you might be interested in. Ha ha! Seriously though. I'm sending you the quote on Monday. Okay then. Ha ha! You're one to talk! Ha ha. Okay now. Au revoir.

In the front hall, Burt stops upon a large fountain. It seems to be a sculpture of a colonial pilgrim pumping water from a tap into some kind of earthenware, held by a Native American woman. Both are smiling gravely.

INT. BURT'S PARENTS' LIVING ROOM — EVENING

In the living room, Gloria is already sitting on the couch, patting the cushion next to her.

> GLORIA
>
> Sit, Verona. Sit next to me and let me hear the heartbeat.

Verona sits.

> VERONA
>
> You can't hear her heartbeat. The placenta's on this side so—

Too late. Gloria has already arranged her head on Verona's stomach. She has one hand on Verona's thigh and the other between her breasts and stomach. Verona would be horrified if she were surprised, but she isn't.

Verona adjusts Gloria's hand a bit so she might be able to feel something. Verona is actually, despite herself, comfortable with Gloria's intimacy.

JERRY, Burt's father, enters the room. He is 55, handsome, successful. He's wearing moccasins and is limping. A self-made man, he grew up working-class and now has achieved an air of incredible suaveness.

> VERONA *(cont'd)*
>
> Hey Jerry! You're looking so much better! You can barely tell.

JERRY

Thank you my dear. Verona, you look . . .
beautific.

Verona and Burt exchange impressed looks—Jerry has a new adjective.

GLORIA

Did you bring the pictures from the sonogram?

VERONA

We did.

Verona tries to get up but Gloria is burrowed into her so deeply that she can't move.

BURT

Here.

Burt removes an envelope from Verona's purse and hands it to Jerry.

JERRY

Oh, these are fabulous.

BURT

You haven't opened the envelope yet.

He hasn't. But now he begins to do so.

JERRY

I can just tell. He's a beauty.

GLORIA

It's a girl.

VERONA
(to Burt)

Did—

BURT

I told you that, Dad.

JERRY

She's a beauty.

Jerry finally gets the envelope open.

JERRY (*cont'd*)

Wow. Spectacular. Exquisite.

Gloria is now laying in Verona's lap.

GLORIA

Jerry, do you want your glasses?

JERRY

I'm fine, Love.

Jerry, struggling without his glasses, is looking at the pictures judiciously, like a doctor examining an X-ray. We cut to a shot of the sonogram, which is horrifying. A straight-on picture of the baby's face, it looks almost exactly like the skull of an alien, with vast ocular cavities and a row of fangs.

JERRY (*cont'd*)

Talk about perfection!

GLORIA

(*looking up from Verona's stomach*)

Do you think she'll look like you?

VERONA

I think so. I'm almost sure I'm the mom.

GLORIA
(*throwing her arm toward Burt*)
I just want a little Verona. After two boys,
I just want a little Verona in a leotard.
Can't you just see her?

Verona pats Gloria's head, which has returned to burrowing into her.

JERRY
(*changing the subject*)
Verona, are you on schedule?

Jerry pronounces the word "shheduuel."

GLORIA
Don't ask her that. Verona, we're just con-
cerned about your tilted uterus . . .

*Verona shoots dagger-eyes at Burt. He looks very surprised that his mom
remembered this detail.*

GLORIA (*cont'd*)
Do you think that might present problems
during delivery?

VERONA
No, I—

GLORIA
You know how I had him—

She points at Burt accusingly.

                    VERONA
I do.

                    GLORIA
In the tub. Had to call 911 it happened so
fast. My water broke, I called the number
and ten minutes later three fireman burst
in the bathroom. You gotta picture me—

                    BURT
No.

                    GLORIA
I'm twenty-three, gorgeous, alone. My
skirt hiked up around my waist, legs
spread, huffing and puffing and then
    *(as she says "*BANG!*" Jerry mimes the crashing
                    open of a door)*
BANG! I'm surrounded by these three huge
men in the uniforms. It's August. So
humid! My blouse is soaked, I'm engorged
with milk—

                    JERRY
    (tired of this story, mocking her gently)
Did they bring their hoses, Gloria?

                    GLORIA
        (ignoring him)
They were all over me. Very capable men—
they knew what to do. One was up here and

another down there, the third one's massaging my . . . my neck. And where was Jerry?
                    (*pause for effect*)
Jerry was at the aquarium.

                    JERRY
          (*very measured, blinking quickly*)
Fish . . . calm me. It was a stressful time.
There was a new beluga at the time. Beautiful creature.

                    GLORIA
The firemen loved that. Where's your husband? He's at the aquarium.

                    JERRY
                (*to Verona*)
Have you seen one, a beluga? You're sort of
a scientist. They're so graceful, soulful—

                    GLORIA
But we had the testosterone covered.
Believe me. Marco alone!

She's momentarily lost in a reverie, thinking of the three firemen, their hands all over her.

                    JERRY
          (*now to himself as much as anyone*)
With the head and the heft and that pale
wet skin I thought I was face-to-face with
Marlon Brando . . .

INT. BURT'S PARENTS' DINING ROOM — EVENING — LATER

Burt and Verona sit at the table eating soup with Burt's parents, who seem to be in a world of their own.

> **BURT**
> So we've been thinking about what kind of birthing experience we want to have . . .

> **JERRY**
> That's terrific.

Gloria busies herself, putting food on the table.

> **BURT**
> . . . and we think we want to limit the amount of people in the room. Or near the room.

> **GLORIA**
> Oh you don't have to worry about that.

> **JERRY**
> Right. No sweat.

> **VERONA**
> We decided that we don't want any video-taping. Sorry Jerry.

> **JERRY**
> Right. I won't. Fabulous.

VERONA

But we really want you to share this with
us. Your presence is really really important.

GLORIA

You are so right. We're so looking forward
to it. We will definitely be there.

JERRY

And the only reason we won't be there is if
we're living in Belgium.

Burt and Verona are dumbstruck. They have no idea what Jerry's talking about. Gloria didn't expect Jerry to spring the news so soon, but she's happy to ride it.

GLORIA
*(sitting forward now and grinning
maniacally)*
Okay. We have news.

JERRY

It's big.

BURT

What is it?

GLORIA

We're leaving in June.

JERRY

We're finally doing it.

BURT

You're leaving in June? The baby's due in July.

JERRY

Right. To Antwerp. City of Light.

BURT

That's not—No you're not.

JERRY

We are. It's going to be superb.

BURT

Don't say that word.

GLORIA

We thought you'd be proud of us. We've been talking about this for fifteen years and now we can finally do it.

BURT

You're leaving a month before the baby's born? You're moving three thousand miles away from your grandchild?

GLORIA

It's more than three thousand miles, isn't it, Jerry?

JERRY

I think so. Double that.

BURT

I can't believe this.

GLORIA

There are planes, Burt.

Verona has slumped back in her chair in disbelief.

JERRY

This is what we've been planning to do
forever, folks. You know that.

VERONA

I didn't know that.

BURT

How long will you be gone?

GLORIA

Just two years.

VERONA

Two years?
          (*disappointed and exasperated*)
You guys!

BURT

Are you selling the house?

JERRY

Well, that's the best part. We were going
to rent out the house, with the help of a
very elegant gentleman named Fareed. But
no one's come forward yet—

VERONA

How long have you been planning this?

GLORIA

Anyway, if we don't get a renter in the next
month, you guys can stay here while we're
gone. You can have the house for the next
two years!

*Jerry is gesturing around him, as if showing the house to his son for the
first time.*

JERRY

Outstanding.

*Verona looks impressed with this idea. Burt, too, softens. They share a brief
daydream of their daughter running through the house, playing on the immac-
ulate lawn, swimming in the pool. The idea grows on them by the minute.*

The phone rings, shaking them from their reverie.

*Gloria goes to the kitchen to answer it. We hear Gloria's excited voice off-
screen. A series of shrieks and "Uh-huh? Uh-huh"s and "No!"s etc.*

*Meanwhile, Jerry has turned to look at a new sculpture in the dining
room—without saying anything, he's begging them to notice it.*

BURT
(relenting)

What is that?

*It's a bronze sculpture/fountain of a young Native American woman,
wearing little more than a cowhide bikini, raising her arms to the sky,
nipples insanely erect.*

JERRY

Magnificent, isn't it? I was wondering when
you'd notice. Twelve-thousand dollars.

VERONA

I can't believe it.

JERRY

I know! She's a Choctaw princess, I'm told.
(*nodding seriously*)
It's important that we honor our Indian . . .
Our ingenious— Our indigentous people.

Gloria returns, barely able to contain her excitement.

JERRY (*cont'd*)

Who was it?

GLORIA

Nobody.

JERRY

Nobody?

GLORIA

Later.

JERRY

Later? Was it Fareed?

GLORIA

Not now.

JERRY

Did he?

GLORIA
(*now unable to contain her glee*)
Yes. The day we leave. The day we leave!

Gloria and Jerry clap and kiss. Burt and Verona stare at them, dumb-founded.

CUT TO:

INT. BURT AND VERONA'S CAR — NIGHT

Driving home from Gloria and Jerry's house.

VERONA

They're very strange people. I always forget how strange they are.

Burt is fuming.

BURT

We can get different grandparents. The second they said "Belgium" I started thinking of ways to hurt them. We'll make someone else the grandparents. Our neighbors. What're their names?

VERONA

I don't know.

                         BURT
They look old enough. We can give them
nicknames and tell the baby that those are
the grandparents. The baby won't know
the difference.

                         VERONA
They knew we moved here for them. I
mean, we've only been here for a year and
now . . . They'll miss the baby's first two
years. It's kinda selfish, right?

This crosses a line with Burt.

                         BURT
It's not like your parents are doing anything.

                         VERONA
My parents are dead, Burt.

                         BURT
Still . . .

They drive in silence.

INT. BURT AND VERONA'S HOUSE — NIGHT

*Verona enters, Burt close behind. She stops after entering, as if seeing their
sad little home with new eyes. It's clearly freezing inside.*

                         VERONA
I can see my breath.

BURT

I'll get the thing.

Burt pulls a space heater out from under Verona's desk. The second he plugs it in, the lights go out; he's blown a fuse.

The house is in total darkness.

BURT *(cont'd)*

Candles.

The opening of drawers. A match is struck. This outtage is routine. Now we see them in candlelight. The conversation continues as they get candles lit all over their small house.

VERONA

You know . . . There's nothing keeping us here.

BURT
(busy with the candles)

Huh.

VERONA

Did you hear me? We could leave, too.

BURT
(still not paying attention)

Right.

VERONA

Burt. I'm serious.

BURT

Fine. Where would we go?

VERONA

Anywhere. We don't have to live here. I
can do my job anywhere, and all you need
is a phone, right? The only reason we're
here is because your parents are here—or
were here.

BURT

We don't want to go back to Chicago, do
we? We did Chicago. And don't say Belgium.

Verona hadn't thought this far.

VERONA

I don't know.

Now Burt is excited by the idea. They continue to light candles.

VERONA *(cont'd)*

I used to picture myself in Alaska. I love
that landscape.

BURT

Alaska! You've never mentioned Alaska.
Wow . . .
      (really excited)
They pay people to live in Alaska.

Verona has already written it off.

VERONA

What about Phoenix? We could live near my sister. Think of that! Oh, that would make me so happy. And Lily and Lowell live there.

BURT
(*almost remembering*)

Who are Lily and Lowell?

VERONA

Lily my boss in Chicago?
(*off his blank stare*)
Red cowboy boots?

BURT

Oh, the "fun" boss?

VERONA

She promoted me. She helped us a lot, Burt. She and Lowell can be our friends in Phoenix.

BURT

But they weren't our friends in Chicago.

VERONA

But they can be in Phoenix. They can be our new good friends when we live in Phoenix.

BURT

We won't need a space heater in Phoenix . . .

They sit for a moment, now surrounded by candles. The scene is oddly beautiful and romantic. Verona slumps back on the couch, defeated.

> VERONA
>
> Burt, are we fuck-ups?

> BURT
> *(adamantly)*
>
> No!
> *(less certain)*
> What do you mean?

> VERONA
>
> I mean, we're thirty-four—

> BURT
>
> —I'm thirty-three—

> VERONA
>
> —And we don't have this basic stuff figured out.

> BURT
>
> Basic like how?

> VERONA
>
> Basic like how to live.

> BURT
>
> We're not fuck-ups.

> VERONA
>
> We have a cardboard window.

She points to a broken window covered with a piece of cardboard.

> BURT
> *(uncertain)*
> We're not fuck-ups.

> VERONA
> *(whispering)*
> I think we might be fuck-ups.

> BURT
> *(even less certain)*
> We're not fuck-ups.

INT. DOCTOR'S OFFICE — DAY

Verona and Burt are waiting for the doctor to come in. Burt is playing with the stirrups.

> VERONA
> I don't want you on that side when the doctor's examining me.

> BURT
> Why not?

> VERONA
> Because you're not a doctor.

> BURT
> *(examining some instruments in the cabinet)*
> Rona, the only thing they've got that I don't is experience.

VERONA
Yeah. Experience at being a doctor.

BURT
(thinking he's won the argument)
Exactly.

DR. HILL *knocks on door and enters. She's young, blonde, with a kind face and bad jewelry.*

DR. HILL
How are you doing, Verona?

Dr. Hill speaks in a slow whisper, as if she's mixing her meds.

VERONA
I'm good.

DR. HILL
Nothing surprising?

VERONA
No, everything's pretty predictable.

A rubber snap draws Dr. Hill's attention to Burt. He's just finished putting on disposable gloves, as if he and Dr. Hill will be performing the exam together.

VERONA *(cont'd)*
This is Burt.

BURT
I'm the husband.

                    VERONA

        He's not my husband.

                    BURT

        I'm the father.

*Dr. Hill looks to Verona to confirm this, which she does with an almost
reluctant closing of her eyes.*

*Dr. Hill smooths gel on Verona's stomach and uses a Doppler to listen to
the baby.*

                    DR. HILL

        Okay. I'd like to listen to baby's heartbeat
        and see if it's as . . .
            (she hesitates, searching for the right word)
        . . . relaxed as it was last time.

*We hear the sounds of the heartbeat. Verona smiles. Burt smiles. Dr. Hill
frowns.*

                DR. HILL *(cont'd)*

        It's still on the slow side. I don't think it's
        anything to worry about. Baby's just . . .

                    VERONA

        It's a girl.

                    DR. HILL

        She's just a little mellow.

                    BURT
              (his face lighting up)
Could it mean she's an athlete? Athletes
have slow heartbeats.

                   DR. HILL
               (dismissively)
No. It's probably a bit soon to know if
she'll be playing sports.
               (turning to Verona)
Um . . . I'm going to do a quick exam
down there.

*Dr. Hill puts on gloves. Burt switches positions so he's standing near
Verona's head.*

                    BURT
                (to Dr. Hill)
She hasn't been able to shave. She can't see
down there and she won't let me do it. But
it's a thicket, right? You almost expect
thorns, blackberries—

                   DR. HILL
        (proceeding with the exam, ignoring Burt)
Well, your uterus has expanded, so it's no
longer tilted.

Verona gives Burt a triumphant look.

              DR. HILL *(cont'd)*
Everything else there is looking good. Nice
job.

VERONA

Thanks.

BURT
(*now taking off the rubber gloves*)
Thanks.

Dr. Hill deposits her gloves in the garbage, and Burt does, too, as if together they've just finished surgery.

DR. HILL

So are you videotaping?

VERONA

What?

DR. HILL

Documenting the stages, the baby's growth, your body changing . . .

BURT

Yeah, I am.

He clearly just got the idea.

VERONA

What about traveling? Is there any reason I can't get on a plane?

DR. HILL

Where are you going? Don't say Dallas.

VERONA

No. Phoenix. And a few other places.

BURT

We're looking for a new place to live.

DR. HILL

Wow. That sounds nice. To get away. To
keep going. Like a quest . . .

*Dr. Hill says the word like a Tolkien wizard would, while staring at the
walls. Instead of medical charts or cheerful pictures, there's a large self-
portrait Dr. Hill has done. It's insanely depressing, seemingly painted
with mud and hay.*

DR. HILL *(cont'd)*

You seem really happy, Verona.

VERONA

I am. I do feel happy. Sort of exuberant.

DR. HILL
(saying the word like it's completely foreign)
Exuberant.
(thinking on it)
Well, be prepared. A lot of people—a lot of
my patients at least—experience a severe
depression after giving birth. There's the
usual baby blues, but then there's the real
deal. It'll drag you through the clouds till
you can't see the sun.

Burt and Verona begin feeling depressed, then and there.

                    DR. HILL *(cont'd)*
Just let me know and I can write you a pre-
scription. Most of my patients are on
Zoloft and they . . . love . . . it.
          (she takes a pad and rips off the top page;
            it's pre-written—she gives the same
                  drugs to everyone)
Actually, here's a script just in case.

She pauses a moment, staring into the eyes of her self-portrait.

                    DR. HILL *(cont'd)*
Just keep the end result in mind. When
you have your baby, it'll be just great.

*There is no way Dr. Hill, or anyone, could have said this in a less con-
vincing way.*

INT. DENVER AIRPORT — DAY (APRIL)

*The AIRLINE DEPARTURES screen lists dozens of destinations, from Hous-
ton to London to Mexico City.*

*Burt and Verona stand in silence on a moving walkway. They seem sud-
denly small and alone as they slowly move through the crowded airport.*

                    BURT
Now I'm wondering what we're doing.

                    VERONA
We're going to Phoenix. On an airplane.
This is where they keep the airplanes.

BURT

But in general. Are we nuts?

VERONA

We'll look around. We agree we need to be
near some kind of family, some friends—
something, some connection, someone we
know. So we'll see Phoenix, see my sister—

BURT

. . . and our new closest friends . . .

Burt can't remember their names. He still has no idea who these people are.

VERONA

Lily and Lowell. And then to Madison for
your job interview.

BURT

My what?

VERONA
(exasperated)
Oh God. Your interview. You're meeting
with Mutual Choice.
(off his blank stare)
To see if they'll give you a better commis-
sion. You set it up.

*Verona removes a small plastic bag full of pre-cut carrots from her bag. She
eats them as they continue talking.*

BURT

So then from Madison we go home?

VERONA

No. Did you look at the itinerary? I stapled
it to your jacket.
(*Burt locates it—it's actually stapled to the
inside of his jacket*)
We go from Madison to Montreal. Montreal's where I think we should live if we
don't live in Phoenix.

BURT

Okay. Montreal.

VERONA

This is exciting, if you think about it.
We're completely untethered, Burt—this
is a dream scenario!

BURT

Yeah!

They travel for a long, awkward moment.

INT. DENVER AIRPORT — DAY — LATER

*Burt and Verona are now sitting at the gate. They look not unlike Dustin
Hoffman and Katharine Ross at the end of* The Graduate: *they've made
a momentous, irreversible decision and now are wholly unsure about it.
Verona is still eating her carrots.*

VERONA

Then again, it seems weird to just decide
on a place and move there.

BURT
(*picking up the slack*)
C'mon! How did the pioneers do it, Rona?
They just spun that globe, picked a spot
because there was gold there, or . . .
wheat . . . and then the whole family got
moving, in their covered wagons and with
their horses and oxen. They traveled through
rain and sleet, over mountains and plains, and
then three-fourths of them died on the way.
(*beat*)
We're just following in their footsteps, honey.

EXT. PHOENIX — DAY

*We see a brief montage of images of Phoenix. Lots of glass, concrete, cars.
No humans on the streets at all.*

INT. RENTAL CAR — PHOENIX — DAY

They're parked at a downtown CIRCLE-K. *Verona is in the driver's seat of
the rental car while Burt is inside the store.*

Verona is on the phone with Lily.

VERONA
Sure . . . That sounds fun. We'll get there.
No problem.

Burt is still in the store, trying on a visor that says PHOENIX IS PHANTASTIC.
*Now he's holding two bottles of wine up to the glass for Verona's approval. She
points to the one on the left.*

EXT. CIRCLE-K PARKING LOT —
        PHOENIX — DAY

Burt emerges from the store with the wine. To comment on the incredible heat of Phoenix, he's walking in slow-motion, as if swimming through molasses. By the time he's near the car, he's on his knees. Verona rolls down the window.

                    VERONA
            (to Burt, who is now laying beside the car)
        You think we can bring wine to a dog
        track?

                    BURT
            (still laying on the pavement)
        What?

                    VERONA
            (pointing to her phone)
        Change of plans. That was Lily. Lowell got
        some bad news and wants to get out of the
        house.

                    BURT
            (standing up)
        To a dog track?

                    VERONA
        Yes.

                    BURT
        Hold on.

He goes back into the Circle-K.

EXT. GREYHOUND TRACK — PARKING LOT — AFTERNOON

Verona and Burt—who is now wearing the PHOENIX IS PHANTASTIC visor—get out of the car and wander up to the complex.

EXT. GREYHOUND TRACK — AFTERNOON

Near the front entrance they find LILY and LOWELL, with their two children. Lily is 40, wearing red cowboy boots which someone has told her look sexy. Lowell is rigid, with a mustache and short, gelled hair. He wears a button-down shirt and shorts that are a size too small. Their children are ASHLEY, 10 years old and a tomboy, and TAYLOR, 6 years old and on the pudgy side. He's wearing a shirt that also says PHOENIX IS PHANTASTIC.

Lily is turning to tuck in Taylor's shirt when she sees Burt and Verona.

> LILY
> *(rushing toward Verona)*
> Oh God, look at you! You're only six months in! Jesus, you're huge. And your face! It's so fat! And did you always have those freckles or are those new? Wow, those are different. Come here and give us a hug! Lowell, come give a hug to the most beautiful woman in the world!

Lowell walks over. He gives Verona an awkward half-hug.

> LILY *(cont'd)*
> Oh c'mon Lowell. Don't be such a pill. He's upset because we didn't get into the club.

59

Lily turns to the kids.

> LILY *(cont'd)*
> Verona and I were desk buddies in
> Chicago! I hired her! At the agency! That
> was before she broke out on her own . . .
> *(to Verona)*
> I still have no idea where you learned how
> to paint the insides of dead people. So fuck-
> ing disgusting, girlfriend!
> *(now to Burt)*
> She's so talented! Our little artiste!

Lowell is holding a half-full plastic cup of white wine. He sees the bottle in Burt's hand.

> LOWELL
> Oh good.
> *(taking the bottle)*
> I was almost out. I'll get an opener.

Lowell gulps the contents of his plastic cup, and chucks it into the garbage.

EXT. GREYHOUND TRACK BLEACHERS— AFTERNOON

In the center of the track, there's a brief ceremony saluting U.S. soldiers wounded and killed in Iraq. A local middle-schooler sings "The Star Spangled Banner."

Taylor is sitting in the front row of the bleachers, holding a Crayola marker and a racing form, circling the dogs he thinks will win. Ashley is sitting apart from him, watching the action on the track, wishing she were living a different life.

There is a smattering of other spectators watching the race.

> VERONA
> So you're in Arizona! You're Arizonans! I can't believe how big the kids are. Taylor's so handsome!

> LILY
> *(laughs skeptically)*
> Well, thanks. We're gonna do something about the ears. You see them? He looks like a trophy. You know what I mean, one of those trophies with the arms on it?

Lily is finding herself hugely amusing. She has been told a few times that she should do stand-up comedy, and in her mind she's constantly testing out her material.

Lily now turns her attention to Ashley.

> LILY *(cont'd)*
> This one has that dyke look.
> *(wrinkling her nose)*
> She walks like a Teamster. Doesn't she? Isn't that weird? She's only ten but I'm sure she's a dyke. Walk for Verona, Ashley. Show us your tough-girl walk. Go butch on us.

Ashley doesn't move or turn around.

LILY *(cont'd)*

Oh now she's shy. And look at her ass—
she's got . . . what is it, Lowell? Junk in the
trunk? She's got junk in her trunk. Looks
like a duffel bag full of bricks. I don't know
if the dykes go for that or not. Burt, you
worked with a lesbian, didn't you?

BURT

(whispering—not wanting the kids to hear
more of the conversation)

Yes, I—

LILY

(louder, defiant)

I can't hear you.

BURT

(now in a louder whisper)

I just . . . don't know if we should be talking like this in front of the kids.

LILY

Oh God. It's just white noise to them.

We see the kids for a second, and it's clear that they're hearing every word.

Lowell has returned with a corkscrew for the wine. He opens the bottle,
pours wine into plastic cups for everyone.

Lowell leads Burt down toward the front fence.

                    LOWELL

What's your line again, Burt? Lily was telling
me but it was all gibberish coming from her.

                    BURT

Insurance.

                    LOWELL

Like life insurance?

                    BURT

Sometimes. Mostly insurance futures.

He reads Lowell's blank expression.

                BURT *(cont'd)*

Well, just as an individual or family might
get insurance, insurance companies need
insurance   themselves . . . It's   a   hedge
against—

                    LOWELL
        (it dawning on him, the whole Matrix)
Dammit, right. Of course it would come to
this.

                    BURT

What?

                    LOWELL

They made us afraid of everything. Insurance for insurance
                    (mocking)
for insurance.

                      63

He shakes his head.

> LOWELL *(cont'd)*
> This country . . . Well, anyway. If this country is shit, everyone else is just the flies on our shit.

The gun pops. The RACE BEGINS. *The dogs rocket past.*

Lowell throws a steely-eyed glare across the greyhound track. He's shaking his head, silently, as if denying the very existence of the track, of Burt, of his own selfhood.

> LOWELL *(cont'd)*
> Watch Number 8. Kahoutek.

Behind them, we hear a shriek of laughter from Verona and Lily. They're catching up, having a great time.

> LILY
> *(throwing her voice over from the conversation she's having with Verona)*
> Hey Lowell, I used to have tits, right? Verona doesn't remember, I don't think. I had nice jugs, right?
> *(indicating her kids)*
> They sucked me dry.

Lowell barely registers hearing her.

> LILY *(cont'd)*
> How the mighty have fallen. I don't even need a bra—now I just tuck 'em into my socks. Are you ready for that, Burt?

Burt smiles, pretending to like Lily's jokes. Lowell still isn't paying her any mind. He's watching the track, in a trance-state. We see his dog is losing—he's fifteen lengths behind any other dog.

> LOWELL
>
> They're never gonna get it.

Lowell continues to stare out at the track.

> BURT
>
> What?

> LOWELL
> *(almost in a whisper)*
> That bone. They'll never get it.

> BURT
>
> Isn't that the point?

> LOWELL
> *(with sudden passion)*
> But what if they did? Even just once? What if just one of those dogs could catch up to it, could take it, wrap his teeth around that bone, could . . .
> *(now almost miming it)*
> . . . hold it in its hands? How do you think that'd feel?

> BURT
>
> Good, I guess—

> LOWELL
>
> Oh, so good. So good.

> (with a steely squint)
> Someday I want to make that happen.
> > (more determined)
> I will make that happen.

The race finishes. All the dogs they cared about have lost.

> LOWELL *(cont'd)*
> Looks like dinner's on you.
> Lowell downs his wine.

> LOWELL *(cont'd)*
> Let's do it.

INT. RESTAURANT ABOVE THE RACETRACK —
LATE AFTERNOON

They're all sitting at a table as the sun sets beyond.

> LILY
> So Burt, you excited about all this?

He looks around approvingly. He thinks she means the dog track.

> BURT
> Yeah, this is the best one I've seen, I think.

> LILY
> No, the baby, dummy. Does this mean you
> guys will finally get married?

LOWELL
(*to Lily*)
They're not married?

LILY
I told you that. Burt wants to, but Verona
doesn't see the point.

LOWELL
Insurance, for one. If anyone, you should
understand that.

LILY
We didn't have insurance when Ashley was
born. Well, we thought we did and then
we didn't. And I couldn't get it—
preexisting condition.

*Burt and Verona are expected to know what this condition is, but they
don't. Lily twirls her finger around her ear.*

LILY (*cont'd*)
I'm crazy.

A wild giggle escapes her mouth.

LILY (*cont'd*)
Or whatever.

VERONA
(*unconvincingly*)
I don't know. I guess I just never gave that
much thought to . . . marriage-marriage.

67

LILY

Well, at the very least, it'll keep you from taking off in the middle of the night when there's trouble.

Lowell is nodding slowly, intensely.

LILY *(cont'd)*

I almost left Lowell about a dozen times. The kids don't know that.

The kids, of course, are right in front of them.

LILY *(cont'd)*

But then you start thinking of the wedding, all that money—

LOWELL

Forty-six thousand for ours. It was worth maybe thirty-one, thirty-one-five . . .

LILY

(sighing happily)

I hope you guys move here. We're having a hell of a time getting into the social world here. Seems very cliquish. I don't know what it is. We didn't get into the good golf club.

LOWELL

(looking away)

No water left anyway. Drought's coming. Like the Biblical flood, but in reverse.

> (slipping into an incantatory tone)
> The golf courses will be the first to go . . .
> Then the fountains, all the water
> fountains . . . Restaurants . . . All the basic
> services . . . Large mammals . . . Then reg-
> ular ones . . . Reptiles, birds . . . Then the
> people.

Long silence. A tumbleweed blows by.

> LILY
> Are you done?

Lowell snaps back to the present. No idea what to say.

> LOWELL
> Thanks for treatin'.

EXT. PARKING LOT OF GREYHOUND TRACK — EVENING

> LILY
> (gushing, utterly sincere, but clearly tipsy now)
> Well, that was wunnerful.

Lowell walks by, throws the wine bottle, now empty, loudly into the garbage can, and heads into the parking lot to find the car. The kids shuffle after him. He says nothing to Burt and Verona—he's either too drunk or has forgotten them completely.

> LILY (cont'd)
> I so hope you move down here. This is the
> place for you guys—it's obvious. Don't listen

to anyone else. And I'm sorry we brought up the marriage thing. You guys do what you need to do. Your baby won't care. Kids are resilient—and they're genetically predetermined anyway; they're screwed up out of the womb—so what. They'll have cell phones. They'll be fine.

Ashley has wandered off and is leaning into the window of a pickup truck—talking to two middle-aged cowboys. Taylor is nearby, picking gum off the hot cement.

LILY *(cont'd)*
Okay here—

She grabs Verona for a goodbye hug and kiss, and then moves onto Burt, who she tries to kiss on the lips. It's quick and clumsy, but tongue is briefly visible. He fends her off and she quickly stumbles away.

EXT. HOTEL POOL, PHOENIX—LATER THAT NIGHT

Burt and Verona are sitting on deck chairs by the pool, positioned side-by-side, very much like sunbathers. It's about 9 o'clock and dark.

BURT
You don't agree with them, do you?

VERONA
(reflexively)
No.
(pause)
About what?

70

BURT

That you can't make a good family, that it's
all bound for failure so—

VERONA

No. I don't.

Beat. The sound of crickets.

VERONA *(cont'd)*

You know I don't agree, Burt. I hate that
attitude—"Everything's broken so let's
*(putting her feet on the ground and stomping, as
        if crushing the shards of a vase into dust)*
break everything again and again and
again."

They stare into the starry sky.

BURT

Did you hear what Lily was saying about
her boobs? Did you know her when she had
boobs?

VERONA

She was huge.

*This is very disturbing news to Burt, but he pretends it's fine. He hadn't
thought of this, and would miss Verona's medium-sized chest.*

BURT

(putting on a brave face)
Well, as long as the baby's healthy, right?

71

INT. HOTEL ROOM — NIGHT — CONTINUOUS

Burt and Verona are moving about the room, unpacking and changing into their sleep clothes.

> BURT
>
> Was your mom . . . Did she breastfeed you and Grace?

> VERONA
>
> I don't know.

> BURT
>
> You don't know?

> VERONA
>
> She died when I was twenty-two. I didn't get around to asking her.

> BURT
>
> Did your mom have . . .

Burt very subtly is indicating breasts with his hands.

> VERONA
>
> She looked like me, Burt. She was medium-sized.

> BURT
>
> After she had you guys, too?

Burt is beginning to brighten.

                    VERONA
Yes.

                    BURT
Cool. Fine. Good to know.

*Verona gives him a look. Now Burt realizes he shouldn't be grinning about
the size of Verona's dead mother's breasts. He stops.*

INT. HOTEL ROOM — NIGHT — LATER

*Burt and Verona are laying in bed, spooning, each looking out the window
at the pulsing highway beyond.*

                    BURT
Um . . .

                    VERONA
          (*knowing he's still stuck on the subject*)
What?

                    BURT
Well, she might not have breastfed you
guys . . .

                    VERONA
Please, Burt.

                    BURT
What?

VERONA

This is the most interest you've ever shown in my mother, and it's about her boobs. It's making me not like you.

BURT
(genuinely so)
Sorry.
(kissing her)
Sorry.
(then back in the saddle)
I just think we need to do the research. I think we need to know what kind of strategies there might be. I mean, I see plenty of older women who still have their boobs. So there must be a way to keep them. You like your boobs, right?

VERONA

Yes.

BURT

So you'd want to keep them if you could . . .

VERONA

Sure.

BURT

Good. So I'll do the research. I'll figure out what it takes. I'm sure there are some guidelines.

Beat. She's curled in bed, her back to him. She's not quite mad at him, but not loving his thinking.

> BURT *(cont'd)*
> Together we'll do this. I'll do this. For
> you—the most sexy lady in the world.
>> *(spooning into her)*
> You're my light, my sky.
>> *(beat, as the idea occurs to him)*
> I can't wait to see you be a mom. Her little
> hand in yours. Your smile on her face.
> They lie for a moment. He hears her crying
> softly.

> BURT *(cont'd)*
> What?

> VERONA
>> *(turning to him suddenly)*
> What are we gonna do?

> BURT
> How do you mean?

He turns her over so they're face to face. She wipes her tears away quickly but her face is soaked.

> VERONA
> No one's in love like us, right? It's so
> weird. What are we going to do?

He wipes her tears, puts his leg over hers, Lennon-style. Soon he has her wedged into his chest.

BURT
(*a whisper*)
I don't know. I guess we just have to ride it
out.

Long moment as they try to sleep this way, face-to-face and entwined.

VERONA
(*whispering, apologetic*)
I can't sleep like this.

INT. RENTAL CAR — DRIVING TO GRACE'S HOTEL — DAY

Burt and Verona are driving to meet her sister, Grace. Grace works as an assistant manager at a very high-end resort hotel in the desert outside of Phoenix. Burt is driving, and this is a problem. He tends to push the accelerator down in bursts, making anyone in his vehicle seasick.

VERONA
This is why I don't let you drive.

BURT
Tell me one more time why we're not stay-
ing at the hotel where your sister works?

VERONA
They've been booked for year. Belgians.

BURT
No. Belgians?

VERONA

Botanists.

As Burt drives the car to the hotel front entrance, he sees three delicate and dour men, clearly Belgian, walking on the sidewalk carrying little comical cacti like offerings.

Burt honks angrily.

BURT

What the fuck with the Belgians all of a sudden? For thirty-three years I have no interaction with Belgians and now they're fucking up every aspect of my life.

Burt honks at another group of Belgians, this batch including some children. They look startled and utterly innocent.

EXT. GRACE'S HOTEL — FRONT ENTRANCE — VALET AREA — DAY

Burt stops the car. Verona adjusts her dress over her belly and turns to Burt.

VERONA

Listen. Grace has been dating this guy named Rob, who seems nice but she thinks he's boring. He likes going to steakhouses, that kind of thing.

BURT

Wait, was that a good thing or a bad thing, the steakhouses?

                         VERONA
Bad.

                          BURT
Like an Outback Steakhouse?

                         VERONA
I'm not sure—

                          BURT
Ruth's Chris Steak House?

                         VERONA
—I honestly don't know. But we need to
make him seem cool. She likes you, Burt.
She'll value your endorsement of this guy.

They get out of the car and make their way through the parking lot. We see
an expanse of desert stretching away behind them.

                    VERONA *(cont'd)*
And don't look at her chest.

                          BURT
I'm over it. I was good last time.

                         VERONA
But she's bigger now. She went on the pill
and now she's complaining about getting
new bras and everything.

They enter the hotel.

                           78

BURT (O.S.)
Why don't you go on the pill?

VERONA (O.S.)
Huh. I wonder . . .

INT. HOTEL LOBBY — LUNCHTIME

Burt and Verona sit in the large lobby of the hotel.

Nearby they spy a MOM *with her two kids, 5 and 18 months. The mother is talking to her kids very loudly, as if everyone nearby should be interested in hearing what she says to her children—and all aspects of her fascinating child-rearing.*

MOM
Yes, Beckett! That's a fern!

Burt and Verona keep watching. Verona is getting annoyed.

MOM *(cont'd)*
Yes, that's a cactus. And the plural of cactus is . . .

BECKETT
Cacti?

MOM
That's right!

VERONA
(to Burt, between her teeth)
Performance moms. Nothing goes un-narrated.

The mom looks around, expecting everyone in the vicinity to smile at the wonder of childhood and her spectacular little family. She finds only Verona, staring her down with a look of unmitigated disgust.

> BECKETT
> (pointing to Verona's stomach)
Baby!

> PERFORMANCE MOM
> (delighted)
Right, Beckett! This woman is about to have a baby—any day now!

> VERONA
Or in three months.
> (giving the mom a fake smile)
Thank you.

The kid is still at Verona's side, inspecting her. The Performance Mom thinks she has an audience and is thus more delighted than ever.

> PERFORMANCE MOM
Beckett, tell the pretty lady what you know about babies.

The boy says nothing. He's frozen up.

> PERFORMANCE MOM (cont'd)
C'mon, tell the nice people.

The boy directs a malevolent look at his baby sister.

> PERFORMANCE MOM (cont'd)
Beckett. You're being rude—

BECKETT
(*still staring at his sister*)
Babies like to breathe and are good at hiding it. I put a pillow over a baby and I
thought she wasn't breathing but then she
was. She was sneaky. She was breathing the
whole time. But I'll try again.

Ashen-faced, the Performance Mom and her kids leave. As they move away, we see Grace coming toward them.

Grace is saying goodbye to a group of Belgians—she speaks a slew of beautiful French with them and approaches Verona and Burt.

GRACE
Holy shit, you're actually showing! I like
that dress.

She throws herself at Verona and they give each other a huge long hug. They release and she sizes up Burt.

GRACE (*cont'd*)
(*pointing to Verona's stomach*)
Burt! Look what you did to my sister!

She gives Burt a quick but very tight hug. She and Verona think nothing of it, but Burt is in a momentary daze.

GRACE (*cont'd*)
So you guys want to eat here, or go
out? . . .

BURT
Oh we don't want to go out there.

GRACE

Yeah, it is pretty hot.

BURT

Feels like we're being cooked. Like God put us here to melt us down and make something better.

GRACE
(*meaning it*)

Wow, Burt. That is so stoney!

BURT

Well, it's the Bible. QED.

EXT. HOTEL PATIO — MIDDAY

Mid-conversation:

GRACE

Two days ago he asked me if I like music. Like music is something some people don't like. He actually posed the question like it was some great conversation-starter.
(*imitating his voice*)
"Grace, I want to ask you something. Do you like music?"
(*looking into her salad*)
It was painful.

BURT

I wish someone would ask me that some-
time. That's a probing sort of intelligence,
I think.

GRACE

Really?

BURT

He doesn't assume the obvious. He's a
lawyer, right?

GRACE

Tax attorney.

BURT

He's gotta be sharp. Gotta be wily.

Verona winces and looks at him: Where does he get these adjectives?

GRACE

He drives a Cabriolet.

BURT

Great design. Good mileage.

GRACE

He uses the word "robust."

BURT

Lots of things are robust!

GRACE

He took me to Long John Silver's.

                    BURT
                  (to Verona)
I thought you said it was a steakhouse.

                   GRACE
When I told him I didn't want the steakhouse, he took me to Long John Silver's.

                    BURT
He's being sensitive to your needs and
desires. This guy seems like a goddamned
champ. He seems awesome. Grace, I need
you to know something. I think you guys
should get married.

*Grace now sees through the gambit. She gives Verona a look that says
"Enough."*

Burt's phone rings. He's relieved.

                 BURT *(cont'd)*
I'm just gonna take this.

*He leaves. Verona and Grace watch him like two moms would watch their
children play.*

                 BURT *(cont'd)*
          (on phone, in loud, Casey Kasem voice)
Ned! I can't believe you're not hiding
under a rock with the way your Titans
played last Sunday!

Burt is momentarily distracted by a large-breasted woman passing by.

                     84

VERONA

Look at him. The baby might have three
hands and a shovel for a head, and he's most
worried about whether or not I'll keep my
boobs.

GRACE

I think that's sexy.

BURT

. . . Ha ha ha! What? Yes siree I had money
on it! Did you get the plan I sent over?

GRACE
(as she watches him)
You got lucky, sister.

*Verona ponders this for a second. She's inclined to cut the compliment with
self-deprecating humor, but she refrains.*

VERONA

Yeah. I know.

As if on cue, Burt trips over a plant.

EXT. DESERT — SUNRISE

The sun rises over the desert.

INT. BATHTUB SHOWROOM — DAY

*Verona and Grace are walking through the aisles, touching the bathtubs
and fixtures. This is a high-end showroom for decorators, and people with
a lot of disposable income.*

VERONA

So what would you think if we moved
here? You could be Auntie Grace all the
time. We could drive Burt crazy.

GRACE

I would love it, Rone. You have no idea.
But I don't know if I'm here for the long
haul. I wouldn't want you moving all the
way here just to see me leave.

VERONA

What about Rob?

GRACE

Be serious. He's already—I called him yesterday. He's . . .
                    (jokingly dramatic)
Part of my past now.

VERONA

So you're going to be a nomad? You're
looking at seven-thousand-dollar tubs!

GRACE

As an investment. I can sell my house for
twice what I paid for it. I can live five years
off the profit. I just might do that . . .

VERONA

Where did you come from? No one else in
our family was good with money.

GRACE

Duh. I've spent years straightening out all
their bank stuff. No one can understand
how economics professors could be so clueless. I'm always like, "They taught revolu-
tionary economics. Not so practical." Dad
paid the bills on the ironing board!

*Grace clearly wants to talk about home and opens her mouth to continue to
do so—but Verona wants just the opposite.*

VERONA
(decidedly changing the subject)
So are you looking for a jacuzzi-type thing
or just a tub-tub?

GRACE
(a bit crestfallen)
Jacuzzi.

They walk through the showroom.

GRACE *(cont'd)*
So do you feel different? You look the same.
I kind of worried you'd have this holy-
mother vibe . . .

VERONA
No, I haven't been . . . tapped on the
shoulder by an angel yet. I don't know.
Maybe I should feel different. Maybe it's
just late coming to me. Everything's late, I
guess.

GRACE

Can you believe Mom was twenty-five
when she had you?

Verona lets this thought fade. Grace knew she would.

GRACE *(cont'd)*

Get in.

Grace sits inside a large white tub set atop giant claw feet.

VERONA

I don't need to get in. It's a nice tub.

GRACE

Come on. I'll wash your hair.

Verona sheepishly steps into the tub and sits with her back to Grace. Grace takes her hair into her hands and kneads it, pretending to lather shampoo into it.

GRACE *(cont'd)*

So . . . when was the last time you went
back home?

VERONA

You know it's been a long time.
(*beat*)
When are you going to sell that place, anyway?

GRACE

You mean when are we going to sell it? I
don't know. Not yet. We've had good luck

with renters. Selling it just seems . . . like
the last thing.

A pause. Verona is getting more reflective.

>   GRACE *(cont'd)*
> It's weird to think the baby won't have
> grandparents from our side.

>   VERONA
> Stop. You're doing it again.

>   GRACE
> What?

>   VERONA
> You're getting all maudlin. You're trying
> to get me to talk about them.

>   GRACE
> That's because you never do.

>   VERONA
> I do. You know I do. I just did.

>   GRACE
> But I want to talk more.
>   *(pause)*
> You're the big sister. You remember more.

Verona accepts this. Just barely.

>   VERONA
> What do you want to know?

Grace doesn't have any specific questions in mind. But the open door gives her strength.

> GRACE
> You know that baby's going to have some-thing of them in her. What if she's got Mom's crazy green eyes or something? What if it's one of those features that skipped you and me and jumps onto the face of that little baby in you?
> *(pause)*
> I can't wait. You're bringing them back, you know? In a little way.

> VERONA
> I know . . .

Verona's misting up.

> VERONA *(cont'd)*
> Are you trying to make me cry? In a bath-tub, in a bathtub showroom?

Grace decides to back off and sum up.

> GRACE
> You're gonna be a great mom. Like our mom.

Pause. We focus on Verona. In the corner of the frame, we see Grace's little finger tap Verona on the shoulder. Verona smiles.

INT. PHOENIX AIRPORT — DAY

Burt and Verona are engaged at the ticket desk. This is a Southwest-type airline, where the employees are encouraged to have "personality."

> TICKET AGENT
> You know you can't fly after eight months.
> Airline policy.

> VERONA
> *(cheerfully)*
> Oh, I'm only six months.

The ticket agent, GWEN, *looks at her skeptically.*

> GWEN
> Dana, come here for a second.

DANA, *another agent, comes over.*

> DANA
> You have a note from the doctor?

> BURT
> What? Really?

> VERONA
> *(to Burt)*
> It's okay. You're supposed to have a note if
> you want to fly after eight months.
> *(to Dana and Gwen, with a tight smile)*
> But I'm six months.

Gwen and Dana both look at her, sure that she's over eight months.

> DANA
> Carrie, you got a minute?

CARRIE, *a third agent, comes over. Now the three of them are looking her over, and Verona is about to explode.*

> CARRIE
> Can you turn to the side?

QUICK CUT TO:

INT. TRAIN STATION — AFTERNOON

Verona has her head down, furious still. Burt is walking behind her down the platform, eagerly.

> BURT
> I think this is better, actually.

Verona is charging ahead, weaving through the crowd, which is parting before her.

> BURT *(cont'd)*
> The railroad! The romance of the rails!

Verona is paying him no mind. At the train, she drops her bag, letting him lift it, and she gets onboard.

BURT (cont'd)
(with boylike wonder, as he gets onboard and
looks back down the train)
Maybe we'll see some buffalo!

INT. TRAIN — EVENING

Burt and Verona are crammed into a small sleeper compartment. Verona is struggling to get onto the bunk.

VERONA
I'm so tired of being big.

Burt helps her up.

VERONA (cont'd)
I'm tired of not having sex.

BURT
Do you want to have sex?

VERONA
No.

Burt stares blankly.

VERONA (cont'd)
We haven't done it in a month.

BURT
But you don't want to now.

                    VERONA
        No.

She looks at him sadly.

                VERONA *(cont'd)*
        . . . I just feel so ugly.

Burt doesn't pick up on the clue, and this annoys Verona.

                    BURT
        So we don't have sex for a while. I was pre-
        pared for that. This is one of those dips we
        go through. There are periods when you
        don't have sex, Rone. I mean, what if I got
        into a horrible boating accident, and was
        covered in third-degree burns on most of
        my body? We'd do without sex then,
        right?

*Verona can't believe this. She grabs an empty plastic water bottle and
heads to the door. She stops.*

                    VERONA
        I'm pregnant, Burt. You didn't get in a
        boating accident. And how do you get
        burns in a boating accident?
                (*opening the door*)
        We don't even HAVE a boat.

                    BURT
        Yeah but—

She closes the door on him.

INT. TRAIN CORRIDOR — EVENING

Relief. We follow her all the way down the silent train corridor, in utter silence. She savors the quiet, the respite from Burt's mouth. She goes to the tap, fills up the water bottle, and when returning, slows down as she comes upon the door, almost knowing that as soon she opens it, he'll begin again—as if the conversation had never paused.

She takes a breath. She opens the door.

INT. TRAIN SLEEPER COMPARTMENT — EVENING

She was right.

> BURT
>
> Funny you mentioned not having a boat. I meant to talk to you about that. I want the baby to grow up knowing the joys of the high seas. I want to raise her on the water. I want the salt water running through her veins!

Verona throws herself onto the bunk and buries her face in her pillow. Burt misinterprets this as a sign that she's still upset about being big.

> BURT *(cont'd)*
>
> Rona? C'mon. Don't be sad. You're not that big. And you're still super-sexy. Hot even.

She buries her face deeper.

> BURT (*cont'd*)
> Oh honey. I'll always love you, even if you're enormous. Even if it takes you MONTHS to lose the weight! A year! I'll love you always, Rone—even if you GAIN weight after the baby.

Verona makes no sign she's hearing him.

> BURT (*cont'd*)
> (*now quieter, as if he's saying something really poignant now*)
> Even if you gain so much weight I can't find your vagina.

She screams into the pillow.

> BURT (*cont'd*)
> (*now whispering*)
> Really. You can write that in stone, in your heart. I . . . will . . . love you . . . even if . . . I can't find your vagina.

INT. TRAIN CAFE — DAY

They are sitting side-by-side in a crowded cafe car, trays down, having just finished breakfast. The landscape outside flashes by, now greener.

Verona, wearing the headphones, is listening to the baby's heartbeat with a portable Doppler machine.

> VERONA
> Her heart-rate is still pretty slow.

BURT

What is it?

VERONA

Like 115.

BURT

That's normal enough, right?

VERONA

It's supposed to be between 120 and 160.

BURT

She's just mellow. Mellow's good.

VERONA

I don't want mellow now. I want lively now, mellow later.

BURT

I think it's fine.

VERONA

It's because you don't want to fight. We should fight more. Get her riled up.

BURT

Didn't we fight last night?

VERONA

We discussed. We need to fight. You never raise your voice.

BURT

Fine. Okay . . . You did something wrong
and I'm bothered about it. Man, am I cross.
Real mad.

VERONA

No. It has to be convincing.

BURT

Should I swear?

VERONA

No. Just raise your voice.

BURT

(suddenly yelling)
You cunt-sucker!

The entire train car turns.

VERONA

(in an urgent whisper)
I didn't mean now!

BURT

But the element of surprise is crucial!
You've never heard me say cunt-sucker,
have you?

Verona has sunk so low in her seat that she's talking into her breasts.

VERONA

No!

                    BURT
         See? I'll get that heart-rate up.
         I know what I'm doing.

He pats her hand. She's still recovering.

EXT. SMALL COLLEGE CAMPUS — DAY

Burt and Verona walk through a tree-filled college campus. They're enjoy-
ing the foliage, the tidiness of it all.

                   VERONA
         This is nice.

                    BURT
                (looking around)
         Yeah . . . Wish we weren't late.

                   VERONA
         I should always drive.

                    BURT
         You should. Remind me to let you drive
         next time I argue that I should drive.

                   VERONA
         So is Ellen a full professor, or an associate
         or? . . . And which side is she on—she's a
         first cousin?

                    BURT
         She's not technically my cousin. Her mom
         was an old friend of my dad's. I have no

idea how. They started calling us cousins
when we were kids. You met her at my
brother's wedding. Dark hair, flowy dress.

                    VERONA
Oh . . . Wasn't there a scene with the
band? Didn't she get in a fight?

                    BURT
The Cuban band.

                    VERONA
Something about Castro . . .

                    BURT
She loves Castro. She used to write him letters, send him pictures of herself in bikinis.

                    VERONA
How do you know this?

                    BURT
I had to take the pictures.

This is news to Verona.

*Burt sees a professorial type—a woman of about 38, with a baby in a
stroller.*

                    BURT *(cont'd)*
Excuse me. You wouldn't happen to know
where Ellen Fisher-Herrin's office is?

PROFESSOR

Ellen Fisher-Herrin.
> (she says the name with a remarkable
> amount of distaste)

Well I do know, as a matter of fact. She's in
William Stone Hall. Room 340.

BURT

Thanks.

They're about to move when the woman adds:

PROFESSOR

If she's not in her office, you'll see her
around. She'll be the mom without the
stroller.

INT. WILLIAM STONE HALL — DAY

They're walking through the halls of the building, looking for the room
number.

VERONA

She doesn't have a stroller? I thought you
said she got some big trust fund.

BURT

She did. Her mother married a Vanderbilt.
Or a Carnegie. Which one did the pants?

Burt and Verona are rushing through the halls of a red-brick college
building.

BURT *(cont'd)*

What time is it?

VERONA

Two-ten.

BURT

Okay. We're an hour late. Hour and a half.
What's our excuse?

VERONA

I blacked out.

BURT

Too dramatic. You can't use that anymore
now that you're pregnant.

VERONA

You blacked out.

BURT

Okay. I blacked out.

*They arrive at the office. On the door, in vinyl letters it says LN FISHER-
HERRIN.*

VERONA

I thought her name was Ellen. What does L
N stand for?

It dawns on Verona that she spelled "Ellen" innovatively: "LN."

VERONA *(cont'd)*

No.

                              BURT
            Please don't say anything.

                            LN (O.S.)
            It's open!

*They open the door to reveal a woman, seemingly topless, standing behind a
desk. The woman has one baby in a sling, and this baby is sucking on her
left nipple. On the desk stands a four-year-old boy. He's sucking on her
right nipple.*

                          LN *(cont'd)*
                            (waving)
            Hello!

The four-year-old peels his lips from the nipple and waves, too.

                        FOUR-YEAR-OLD
            Welcome!

LN *gestures them forward. Burt and Verona are frozen. LN is about 35,
with luxuriously curly hair.*

                              LN
            Come in, come in. Give me kisses!

INT. LN'S OFFICE — DAY

Verona and Burt proceed, their feet leaden.

*LN tucks her breasts back under her blouse and charges toward Burt and
Verona. The four-year-old wipes his mouth with the back of his hand.*

LN

How are you two? How great to have you
here! I thought something might have
been wrong when you were so late.

BURT

Sorry about that. I blacked out.

LN

How inventive!

She hugs Burt and turns her attention to Verona.

BURT

I can't remember if you guys met . . .

LN

Of course! How could I forget this GOR-
GEOUS woman. Oh Verona! What a
beauty you are. Look at your hair . . .

VERONA

Yeah . . .

LN examines Verona's belly.

LN

And it's a boy.

VERONA
(super-politely)
A girl. Actually.

No, really? With hips like that and the
shape . . .
(she's massaging the stomach quickly, noting its
roundness)
Who told you it was a girl?

VERNA

Um, the doctor. And the sonogram—

LN

Well, we'll see.

BURT

I'm sorry we're a little late. We tried to
call.

LN

Oh, I never answer the phone when I'm
feeding. Not fair to the children . . .
C'mon.
(getting her bag and gesturing toward
the four-year-old)
I have to get this one to crafting.

The four-year-old puts on what seems to be a coat—no, it's a cape, black
and velvet—and they all leave the office.

EXT. CAMPUS—DAY

They're walking through the quad, on the way to their cars. LN is still
carrying the baby in the sling and holding hands with the four-year-old.

They walk past a protest—dozens of students with signs (THE CIA TRAINED BIN LADEN) objecting to CIA recruiting on campus.

> BURT
>
> We got directions from a woman. She seemed to know you. A blazer, brown hair. She had a baby, very tall?

> LN
>
> Ruby. Poor Ruby. She hates me. I breastfed her baby.

> VERONA
>
> Pardon?

> BURT
>
> Is that allowed?

> LN *(cont'd)*
>
> I was babysitting and the child was fussing—he was starving, and he wouldn't take the bottle. So I fed him. Took to me right away. I shouldn't have told her; she didn't appreciate it. She has lactation problems. Now she won't let me babysit, or get near her husband. How paranoid is that? So should we eat in? Out?

Verona is surprised, but Burt doesn't register LN's trespass as clearly.

> BURT
>
> How about in? We've been eating train food.

> LN
>
> Train food. Okay . . . Let's think of what I have at home . . .

VERONA

Let us get the food! We have a car. We can
get the groceries. It's the least we can do.

They've arrived at a parked Prius.

LN

Oh that's great. Look at you, so helpful!

LN steps away from Verona and puts her arm around Burt. They're both
facing Verona now, and LN is talking to Burt as though Verona is on dis-
play to them.

LN *(cont'd)*

You really struck gold. I mean behold this
woman. She's extraordinary. I'm proud of
you Burtie. Well done!

Verona is smiling awkwardly, waiting for the situation to end.

LN moves closer to Verona now, and is touching her arm, as though they're
longtime friends exchanging confidences.

LN *(cont'd)*

I'm so glad you two got pregnant so easily.
To be honest, I had my concerns, given
your tilted uterus. Well, this is me.
(*indicating her car—the Prius*)
You have the directions I e-mailed, yes? I'll
see you at the house.

INT. RENTAL CAR — ON WAY TO GROCERY
    STORE — DAY

Verona is driving. Fuming. The Doppler sits between them.

                    VERONA
                    (furious)
        You told her I have a tilted uterus?

                    BURT
        I don't know. It might have been my mom.
        Is your tilted uterus a secret?

                    VERONA
        Yeah my tilted uterus is a fucking secret!

Something occurs to Burt.

                    BURT
        Oh really, you fucking bitch? Your fucking
        uterus is a motherfucking secret? Well
        fuck you!

Verona is shocked. Burt grabs the Doppler.

EXT. LN'S HOUSE — LATE AFTERNOON

*Burt and Verona walk up the steps of LN's house. They've brought a new
stroller with them as a gift. It's fully assembled, and Burt wheels it off to
the side of the porch so they can surprise LN with it.*

                    BURT
        Can't believe how much this thing cost.

                    VERONA
        Told you. You think it's an okay one?

Burt rings the doorbell.

                    BURT
        They're coming from zero. They'll
        be thrilled.

LN opens the door, wearing a long flowing hippie robe-dress.

                    LN
        Namaste!

Blank looks from Burt and Verona.

INT. LN'S HOUSE — LATE AFTERNOON

They step inside. Sitar music is playing. We see that there's an elaborate cubbyhole set-up for shoes and slippers.

                    LN
        If you don't mind . . .

Verona picks out a pair of black knitted slippers. Burt is left with one option: an elf-like pair, with pointed toes.

                    VERONA
        Here, we brought you something.

Burt goes back to the porch to retrieve their present.

LN
(to Verona)

That is so sweet. Aren't you a dumpling?

From behind the door, Burt reveals the STROLLER, *topped with a red ribbon.*

LN looks at it like a rolling mound of pig shit is coming toward her.

LN *(cont'd)*
(offended but also slightly amused)

Oh no no . . . Please . . . That's not . . .

(letting out an amazed whistle)

Oh wow. Just, uh, leave that on the porch
there.

Burt, thinking she doesn't want the stroller in the house for cleanliness reasons, strolls it outside.

LN *(cont'd)*
(watching him)

Just a little farther . . . Great.

(now rising above)

Okay, why don't you come inside and meet
Roderick. He's upstairs.

INT. FAMILY BEDROOM — LATE AFTERNOON

Burt and Verona enter a smallish, dimly lit, wood-paneled bedroom, dominated entirely by a huge mattress. It's almost twice the size of a king-size bed.

110

                              LN
        Hi babe.

It wasn't clear at first, but RODERICK, *LN's partner, is laying on the bed.
Roderick is tall, lanky, with longish dirty-blond hair and a broad open
face. He turns over and greets them with a lazy wave.*

                           VERONA
        Hi.

                            BURT
        Hi. I don't think we've met.

*Burt tries to crawl over the bed on his knees, to shake Roderick's hand.
Roderick makes almost no effort.*

                          RODERICK
        Yes we have. Burning Man. 1997.

*Verona looks at Burt, aghast. Burt quietly acknowledges that this is true.
Backing off the bed, Burt almost steps on Wolfie, the older of the two kids,
who we see is napping, too.*

                            BURT
        Wow, this is a big bed.

Off Burt's blank look.

                              LN
        This is Continuum home.

                           VERONA
        What is that—continuum?

RODERICK
(slightly incredulous)

Continuum?

VERONA

Yes.

LN

Continuum.

VERONA

Yes.

*LN looks to Roderick as if to say "'Are you going to tell them or shall I?'"
Roderick continues with some effort.*

RODERICK

The Continuum movement recognizes that the world will give your baby plenty of alienation and despair in good time, so while we can we should hold them close.

LN

So . . . the three S's. No separation, no sugar, no strollers.
(she turns to Roderick)
They bought us a stroller.

RODERICK
(amused)

No!

BURT

What's wrong with strollers?

Burt. I love my babies. Why would I push
them away from me like that?
  (demonstrating with an aggressive move of
    pushing a stroller, as if off a cliff)
Why do you think this country is so dys-
functional?

VERONA

Because of strollers?

LN

Mama. In this house we carry the children.
We keep them attached. We don't sever the
biological ties at first opportunity.

BURT

What about sleeping?

RODERICK

This is where they sleep. We practice family bed. Sleep-time is their most fraught
time, when they most need to know that
their progenitors are near.

VERONA

What do you guys do when you want to . . .
be alone? Do you go to the car or? . . .

LN
    (with enormous pity)
Oh, Verona, you are precious. No, we don't
go out to the car.
    (turning to Burt)

Are you planning to hide your lovemaking
from your kids? Since when are you so
bashful?

> *(to Verona)*

Do you know what that does to a child, to
have their parents' expression of love kept a
secret from them?

RODERICK

That's why I have an Electra Complex.

BURT

> *(to Verona, under his breath)*

Which one is that again?

VERONA

That's when a woman wants to do her father.

> *(to Roderick)*

Do you mean Oedipal Complex?

RODERICK

Don't diagnose me, Verona.

*Burt and Verona take in the room. There are about two-dozen pictures of
seahorses on the walls. One is carved from teak.*

BURT

Why the seahorses, Rod?

Roderick and LN share a knowing look.

LN

In the seahorse community, the males give
birth.

She gives Roderick a sympathetic look, as if to apologize.

> RODERICK
>
> The female inserts her ovipositor into the male's brood pouch. That's where she deposits her eggs.

> LN
> *(to Roderick, with such tenderness)*
> If I could, I would lay my eggs in your brood pouch.

She leans across the bed to stroke his cheek.

> RODERICK
> I know you would.

Roderick grabs her hand, and passionately sucks her finger.

CUT TO:

INT. LN'S HOUSE — DINNER TABLE — EVENING

At dinner, Verona, Burt, Roderick, and LN are joined by LN's son, WOLFIE, *the four-year-old. They're eating some kind of spicy soup. It's extremely hot, and both Burt and Verona are experiencing some difficulties with it.*

> LN
> It's so good to have you two here.

VERONA
(looking at the placemats, which look like
abstract watercolors)
These are very unusual.

LN

Wolfie and Neptune helped make them.
Didn't you, Wolfie?

Wolf nods proudly.

RODERICK
Placenta transfers. Every one of them's different. That's archival paper—museum
quality.

LN
I can't believe people throw them away.

VERONA
The placenta? Did you eat it?

Burt winces into his soup.

LN
No we didn't eat it, sweetie. We're not bar-
barians.

WOLF
(to Burt)
Would you like a dolma?

BURT
What is it?

                    WOLF
It's an amuse-bouche.

                    BURT
What?

                    WOLF
It means "pleasing to the mouth." To whet
your appetite.

                    BURT
Okay. Right. Thank you.

He takes one.

                    LN
Have you decided on a doula?

                    BURT
        (holding up the appetizer Wolf gave him)
I have one. Delicious.

                    LN
A doula, not a dolma.

                    VERONA
We're not using a doula.

                    LN
A midwife?

BURT

(finally catching on)

No. No. Midwives and doulas are for when the husband is clueless or doesn't want to be involved.

Verona shakes her head, disagreeing.

BURT *(cont'd)*

I am neither of those things. I really want to be involved. And I have a knack for medical proced—

LN

But don't you think Verona might need someone who really understands the female experience? I can't remember the book, but there's a marvelous passage in Simone de Beauvoir . . . "One is not born but becomes a woman." . . .

VERONA

What does that have to do with?—

LN

(gazing at Wolf)

. . . but it's worth it. The pain is so enlightening. Having experienced childbirth, I really comprehend suffering in a new way. Now when I watch CNN, I understand war on a whole new level. On top of which, when I had Neptune, I had the most enormous orgasm.

RODERICK

Sensational.

A stunned pause.

LN
(to Burt)

So how's Jerry?

BURT

My parents are fine, LN. They're moving to
Belgium.

LN

Belgium? Whose idea was that? Sounds
like Gloria's.

*She says "Gloria" with unmistakable scorn, as if she were a competitor of
some kind.*

BURT

What does that mean?

LN

Uncle Jerry was always more of a romantic.
He wouldn't have chosen Belgium. Don't
tell me they're going to Antwerp.

BURT

Just stop. You're way inappropriate about
my dad. And don't call him Uncle Jerry.
He's not your uncle. Just . . . gah.

VERONA

Burt—

BURT

Dammit, LN, you've always done this. You
and your mom always got too involved in
my family. We really—just don't give us
advice about the birth, okay?

VERONA

(trying to change the subject)

This soup is delicious.

RODERICK

Alice Walker says there's nothing more
important than how you enter this world,
and I agree with her. My mom had a hospi-
tal birth—the stirrups, the drugs, the
machines. And she wonders why I can't
walk into a dry cleaners without vomiting.
When I'm twelve she catches me with
some peyote and I'm like, "What'd you
expect? You started it with the epidural."

BURT

Okay, can that, please, be the last of the
parenting-advice portions of the evening?

LN

(to Burt)

So are you counting on this job interview
tomorrow? At . . . Where is it?

BURT

Mutual Choice. Not really. I already do
fine. This would just be a better commis-
sion rate.

*Roderick makes a point to be yawning at the mention of insurance and
interviews and commissions. Burt sees it and ignores him.*

BURT *(cont'd)*

What do you do, Roderick?

RODERICK
(with contempt)

You mean, how do I "make" my "living"?

BURT

What?

LN
(to Wolf)

Don't worry, Wolf. You won't ever have to
do that kind of thing.

BURT

"That kind of thing?"

RODERICK

You know—skimming, billing, fear-
mongering . . .

VERONA

Are you people serious?

LN

Roderick, honey, stop. It's so easy to forget
how great the economic divide is these
days.

(indicating Burt and Verona)

These people have nothing. How can we
expect them to know anything about anything?

(turning to Verona and placing her hand
on hers)

And Verona lost her parents. How old were
you when they passed?

VERONA

(after a long pause)

Twenty-two. Why?

LN

You poor thing. I just wondered how much
your mama had passed onto you about
motherhood. Your people have such a wonderful oral tradition—

Verona, eyes welling, is speechless.

BURT

(slamming his fist on the table)

Ok, that's it. That's it. You people . . .

He stands up. He doesn't have the words..

BURT (cont'd)

You're a terrible person, LN. You always
were. My parents always said—When we

122

were kids— And Verona's twice the
woman . . . And THIS GUY—
>   (*pointing to Roderick*)
Look at him! Just—gah!

He leaves. Verona follows.

>   LN
> What is happening?

>   BURT
> If you can't tell, loony tunes . . . Just—

LN finally realizes that they're really leaving. Burt and Verona are putting on their shoes.

LN and Roderick haven't left the table.

>   LN
> Whatever. Fly away Burtie.
>   (*getting angrier, slipping into a nasty,*
>   *gutteral voice*)
> And TAKE THAT SHITTY STROLLER
> WITH YOU.

As Burt is following Verona down the steps—with the stroller—and now he pauses. An idea comes to him. He turns around.

INT. LN'S HOUSE — EVENING

A second later, like an ax-murderer in the climactic scene of a horror movie, Burt comes barreling into the house, ramming the stroller through the front door. He does a wheelie with it, making a deafening motorcycle sound.

> BURT
>
> Whaaaaaaaaaaaaaaa!

He knocks over a fern and an African totem. The cat squeals and flees out the door.

> LN
>
> No! No!

> BURT
>
> Yes! The stroller has returned! The stroller! Hahahahahahahahah!

It's pandemonium. Wolf screams gleefully.

> LN
>
> Get out of here!

It's pandemonium.

> BURT
>
> Neptune! C'mere! Uncle Burt's gonna PUSH you! In the STROLLLLER! Hahahahahaha!

The kids are screaming and laughing. Verona is in hysterics.

> LN
>
> Roderick, you shouldn't witness this. Go to a safe place.

Roderick goes to the corner of the living room and puts on a cloak—as if it makes him invisible.

> LN
> *(to Roderick)*
> Do your breathing!
> *(to Burt)*
> You bastard!

Burt chases LN and the kids till they close a glass door between them. She thinks they're safe.

> BURT
> Rum-rum-RUM! Come out, and have your Continuum . . . DIScontinued! Ha ha ha ha! And BWAHAHAHAHAHAHA!

> LN
> Think of the children!

As Burt's been talking, Wolfie has run around and is now with him, jumping up and down.

> LN *(cont'd)*
> Wolfie!

Burt, conspiratorially with Wolfie, crouches down so only the stroller is visible.

BURT

(now in an evil falsetto meant to be the voice of
the stroller itself)

Burt is gone but I remain, LN! It is I, the
Stroller! Ah hahahahahaha! And bwahaha-
hah—I never sleep! I only lurk, awake and
watching, waiting for my chance to
STROLL families into disharmony and
dysfunction! Bwahahahahaha!

The kids are loving it.

Burt finally leaves, jumping down from the porch, joining Verona as they
run down the street like bank robbers.

INT. MUTUAL CHOICE OFFICE — NEXT DAY

Burt is mid-interview. MR. BERNARD is about 55, African-American.
He's a kind-faced middle-manager, settled, content.

MR. BERNARD

. . . you know, I saw you play ball. Your
dad took me to a game, the high school all-
star thing in Denver. You were good. I
thought I'd be watching you on ESPN
someday.

Burt notices that on Mr. Bernard's desk there's a digital picture frame,
where the images rotate. There's a progression in place, from Bernard's
marriage photos, to newborn photos, to the growing family (three kids), to
grandkids . . . It's like watching a chronological slideshow, comical in its
perfection.

126

BURT

Yeah, well . . .

MR. BERNARD

But insurance is a noble field, Burt. Nothing to be sorry about. You're providing peace of mind. That's a profound comfort as a family grows.
(*noticing Burt's noticing his photos*)
That's mine. You're married?

BURT

(*awkward; he doesn't want to explain it to this kindly man*)
I . . . Uh . . . We're having a baby.

MR. BERNARD

That's marvelous. When's the due date?

BURT

July. I think the seventeenth.

MR. BERNARD

You think the seventeenth! This is the biggest day of your life! Next to your wedding day!

BURT

(*convincing himself*)
It is the seventeenth. I'm sure of it.

MR. BERNARD

Baby's room ready?

BURT

The what? No. Not yet.

Burt sees Mr. Bernard's surprise and decides to lie.

BURT *(cont'd)*

We're renovating it. We just finished the
canopy bed and this amazing mural, so
we're waiting for that to dry before . . .
> *(making it up as he goes)*

. . . what's taking really long is the climb-
ing wall . . .

Mr. Bernard is slightly confused but doesn't pursue it.

MR. BERNARD

So what part of town are you living in?

*Long pause as Burt watches the family pictures and decides he can't fib
anymore.*

BURT

We're not actually living here.

MR. BERNARD

You're not?

BURT

We're . . . looking right now. Generally for
a place to live—like a place in the country.

MR. BERNARD

The country? Madison isn't the country.

BURT

No I mean, the country of . . . The United
States.

*Now Mr. Bernard understands. He gets up from his desk and sits in the
chair next to Burt. He gives him a sympathetic look.*

MR. BERNARD

Burt, I like you. I'm gonna send your name
up the ladder. I'll let you know something
next week. And by then you'll probably
have more of this other stuff figured out.
Right?

BURT
(without convincing anyone)
Right.

INT. HOTEL ROOM — LATER THAT AFTERNOON

*Verona is packing to leave for the airport. Burt comes in fresh from the
interview and maybe a walk he took afterward. He's still raw, feeling
beaten.*

BURT
(taking off his tie and jacket)
I don't think Madison is good for us. I'm
sorry I brought you here. Did I say I was
sorry about LN and Roderick?

VERONA

Many times.

129

BURT

I don't know what I was thinking.

VERONA

So the interview—

BURT

It was good. It was nothing. He's sending
my name up the ladder.

*Burt is standing, now packing his suitcase, which rests on the bed. Verona
sits down next to it, putting herself in his line of vision.*

VERONA
*(poking fun at the ladder reference
but not at Burt)*
I'm sure it's going right up to the top rung
of the ladder. Or the rung below that
one—you're not supposed to step on the
top one.

*Now Burt wants to change the subject. He sees the video camera in the cor-
ner of the suitcase and pulls it out.*

BURT

We've haven't been documenting.

VERONA

What? Now?

*Verona's initial reluctance gives way to her knowing that he needs this
right now.*

130

VERONA *(cont'd)*
How dirty do you want it?

BURT
Get naked. Up against the window there,
with the light.

Verona complies.

INT. HOTEL ROOM — AFTERNOON — MOMENTS LATER

Verona's undressed and standing near the window, with a soft light falling on her curves.

BURT
That's nice. Nice. Now stand on the chair.

VERONA
What? No.

BURT
Please? You want it to look artistic, don't
you? Stand on the chair. Like this.
(indicating one leg up, like a flamingo)

VERONA
Like a flamingo.
(he nods; she complies)
This works for you?

Soon she's in the desired position, and Burt gets the video camera ready.

131

So glad I brought the tripod.
>   *(getting it ready)*
Ready?

VERONA

I guess. This can't be looking normal to you.

Burt turns the camera on. His eyes go wide.

BURT

Oh Jesus.

VERONA

What?

Through the viewfinder, we see that there's a tape already in the camera. The frame shows a very un-pregnant Verona, naked, standing in much the same position as she is at the moment. The contrast is interesting: in the video, the color is lurid and cheap. Just beyond, in the hotel room, Verona is illuminated softly, and looks ethereal.

VERONA *(cont'd)*

What is it?

Burt is watching, eyes popping.

VERONA *(cont'd)*

You didn't bring that tape.

BURT
>   *(in quiet awe)*
It's in the camera.

Verona comes down off the chair and around to Burt. Together they slowly sit down on the edge of the bed.

VERONA

Oh God. I haven't seen this since we made it.

Burt and Verona sit attentively on the edge of the bed. The tape begins. It's a homemade sex video. The camera has been left on a bookshelf by their bed, and has captured Burt and Verona engaging in a relatively standard sex session.

We watch Verona and Burt as they watch the tape, and the look that comes over their faces is one of utter melancholy. They miss those days.

Barbara Streisand singing "The Way We Were" begins, wall-to-wall. "Memories . . . Like the pages of my mind . . . "

Verona and Burt both begin to get teary.

INT. AIRPORT SHUTTLE — EN ROUTE TO MONTREAL — AFTERNOON

Music continues, wall-to-wall.

Verona is sitting on the shuttle, alone, peaceful. The seat next to her— Burt's—is unoccupied.

We see that Burt is finishing putting the luggage in the racks near the front. Then he starts making his way to the back, using the subway-straps above to keep his balance.

It's romantic, as he keeps his eyes locked on her, weaving through the other travelers toward her. All in semi-slow-motion.

When he finally gets to her, his face suddenly becomes a scowl and his mouth opens into a cave of foul words. He barks out something awful—inaudible under the soundtrack—and as everyone on the shuttle turns and stares, he grabs for the Doppler and the headphones.

EXT. MONTREAL HOUSE—LATE AFTERNOON

Verona and Burt are outside a beautiful walk-up in a clean and charming neighborhood of the city.

> VERONA
> Holy shit. This is their house?

> BURT
> Wow. The mailbox even.

He points to a mailbox, in the shape of a house, with their name on it.

> VERONA
> We went to the same college as these guys.
> How can they be so grown up while we're . . .

> BURT
> Stunted? Confused? American?

They ring the doorbell. The chime is a novelty—the sound of a mild electric shock, and someone reacting to it:

> DOORBELL
> Zzzzt. Ahhh!

Burt plays with the doorbell for a minute—Zzzzt! Aaaaaah! Zzzzzzt! Aaaaaah! The door opens.

We see a five-year-old girl. She's in her pajamas.

> BURT
>
> Hey Camille. Cammie. Remember us?

She shakes her head. Burt is mildly hurt.

> VERONA
>
> Should we come in?

> CAMMIE
>
> Okay. They're in their room. Mom's gonna
> wear a little skirt.

INT. MONTREAL HOUSE/FAMILY ROOM—LATE AFTERNOON

Cammie leads them into the house and into the family room, where everything seems to be happening at once. There's a slide in one corner, a card table with a giant half-done jigsaw puzzle on it, a model aircraft carrier in progress . . .

> CAMMIE
> *(leading them toward the TV)*
> It's almost over.

The Sound of Music is on, and it's at the point where the Von Trapp children perform their "So long, farewell," song.

Cammie rejoins her big brother IBRAHIM, *an Ethiopian adoptee of seven, who's standing in front of the TV in his underwear. The two kids do the dance in time with the music. It's ridiculous-and cute and funny, given the contrast between these two kids and the would-be Aryans onscreen.*

Behind them on the couch is JAMES, *16 and white; nearby, with her legs draped over him, is* KATYA, *10, an adoptee from Russia wearing a huge rainbow wig.*

James waves to Burt and Verona, not wanting to interrupt the kids' dancing. The kids now see Burt and Verona as stand-ins for the dignitaries at the Von Trapp party on screen, and direct their dancing to Burt and Verona.

As Burt and Verona are standing and watching the show, TOM *comes from a back hall and quietly greets them. They all hug.*

Tom is about 34, dark-haired, casually handsome. He's a carpenter-contractor who's done well, primarily because he's honest, decent, and means what he says.

> TOM
> (*just above a whisper*)
> Heeeeey!
>> (*to Verona*)
> You look amazing, Verona. Perfect.

They all turn to watch the kids.

The part in the movie occurs when the kids say goodbye to the partygoers and they all say goodbye back, in unison.

BURT & VERONA & TOM
(singing)

Good bye!

Just then, right after the "Good night" song, the movie ends. Tom mouths "Sshh" to Burt and Verona. Credits roll.

VERONA
(lowering her voice)

So the movie ends when the Von Trapps go
to sleep?

TOM
(also in a quieter voice)

We sorta skipped the rest.

VERONA

You skipped the Nazis?

TOM

Yeah. We kinda figure, What's the point,
you know?

BURT

They haven't caught on?

TOM

Not yet. You won't tell them?

BURT & VERONA

No.

                    TOM
              (*genuinely relieved*)
Thanks man. I appreciate that. There are
always people who want the kids to know
it all right away, the sex and genocide,
everything. We think they can live a few
more happy years before, you know, Juicy
Couture and Hitler.

*There's a little voice that says "Ahem." They all turn around and are con-
fronted with a little face, Cammie's, peaking out of a raincoat. She's suddenly six feet tall.*

                   CAMMIE
Excuse me. Do you know the way to San
Jose?

*Tom throws open the raincoat to reveal Katya below—Cammie's on her
shoulders.*

                    TOM
                 (*to the kids*)
Where'd you get that?
              (*to Burt and Verona*)
They've never done that before.
        (*to the kids, as they're disassembling*)
Well done.

The kids are all giggling.

               TOM (*cont'd*)
Everybody, this is Verona and Burt. Your
mom and I went to school with them.

There are some scattered hellos.

Ibrahim has a Star Wars *rebel fighter ship,* Empire Strikes Back–*era, which he begins to fly around Burt's legs. Soon he has him tied up like an Imperial Assault Walker. Burt plays along, falling in dramatic fashion.*

Meanwhile, Katya and Cammie are holding hands around Verona's belly and circling around her. They're giggling and singing a song they've made up, the chorus of which is "Bun in the Oven." Verona can't move.

KATYA
Do you really draw dead bodies?

VERONA
Sort of.

TOM
I told them about your job.

Now Ibrahim joins them, with one hand down his pants and the other holding the rope that still binds Burt.

IBRAHIM
(to Verona)
I can dismember this prisoner. Then you
can draw him.

MUNCH *trundles down the stairs. She's pretty, curvy, with dark liquid eyes. She has an MBA but has put her career on hold. She puts off a sense of perpetual warmth.*

She's half-dressed in a skirt and high-heels and a sweatshirt over it all. She's installing an earring.

MUNCH

Hi hi hi hi hi! I'm not ready!

She hugs and kisses Verona.

MUNCH *(cont'd)*

Verona, you look so good. I can't believe
you're six months in!

*She seems genuinely happy for Verona, but is overplaying her enthusiasm a
notch.*

MUNCH *(cont'd)*

(to Burt who is still hog-tied up on the ground)
You okay?

BURT

Yeah. I have the same equipment at home.
I do this to relax.

*She reaches down to ruffle his hair in greeting, and sees her raincoat on
the floor.*

MUNCH

(to Burt and Verona)
Did Tom show you your room?

TOM

I was about to.

MUNCH

It's down the hall . . . Will you do that,
Tom? What time is it?

> *(to the adults)*
> We should hustle.
> *(to the kids)*
> Okay, Bigs give Littles a bath! I'll start the
> water.
> *(half to herself, while running upstairs)*
> I should have put the heels on last . . .

James gets off the couch and stands by the stairs. The kids run by him, on their way up. When they're all up, James follows.

TOM

Hey James?

James stops.

TOM *(cont'd)*

We'll be back late. Lock up and give Katya
her medicine? And you have my cell.

JAMES

I do. Have fun.

He disappears upstairs.

VERONA

Who's that? You would have been about
eighteen . . .

TOM

James? He's a stray. Lives down the street.
His dad's a meth addict. Good kid.
Worked on our crew over the summer,
good with wood, drywall, and . . .

>   *(as if it just occurred to him)*
> I guess he lives with us now.
>   *(heading down the hall)*
> Let me show you the room—

There's a sound in the kitchen, someone looking for something.

>   TOM *(cont'd)*
> That's Ibrahim. Looking for his snorkle stuff.

>   VERONA
> Go.

>   TOM
>   *(gesturing)*
> It's at the end of the hall.
>   *(with a shrug)*
> It's a room, right?
>   *(backing up, toward the kitchen)*
> We'll meet you out front in ten?

EXT. MONTREAL HOUSE — EVENING — 10 MINUTES LATER

Burt and Verona are outside, changed and ready to go out.

>   VERONA
>   *(rapturously)*
> This is the family I want. Every part of it. All those kids, all those ages all taking care of each other—

BURT

So you want to adopt?

VERONA

Yes!

BURT
(pointing to her stomach)
What about this one? Should we trade
her in?

VERONA

No. I want her, and them, too. I want to
live in a big house like this, with the
couches, everyone draped over each other,
dancing in their underwear. This is a family.

BURT

Yeah. It works. It's real.

VERONA

We should move here. Montreal. These
guys'll be our best friends and our daughter will be friends with all these kids.

*Tom and Munch pull up in their car, an old convertible. Munch is dressed
up. Tom is wearing driving gloves. They're very serious about a night out.*

TOM

Let's do this.

INT. TOM'S CAR — EVENING

Tom drives very fast. Verona and Burt are in the back seat. The passengers are passing a flask around. Music blares.

VERONA

So you still find time to go out?

MUNCH

We're out a lot, I guess. Depends on when. You have to find that balance. I mean, the kids want you there, but not all the time. They need air as much as you do.

BURT

I think we're moving here.

TOM

To Montreal? We already won the competition? Over Madison? Over Phoenix? Hell yeah!

MUNCH

That's wonderful news.

TOM

Let's toast. Does anyone know a toast?

No one knows a toast.

MUNCH

Okay. So . . . Yay for Burt and Verona moving here. Probably if they're not stupid.

They all cheer.

INT. JAZZ CLUB/BAR — NIGHT

They're at a casual bar, while a jazz combo plays in the background. Tom and Burt are doing shots, a little drunk. They lean back against the bar and turn toward the band.

> TOM
>
> Man, I love the trombone.

> BURT
>
> I was about to say that. The same thing.

> TOM
> *(yelling to the band)*
> More bone!

> BURT
>
> Bone!

INT. JAZZ CLUB TABLE — NIGHT — SIMULTANEOUS

> Munch and Verona are having a private talk.

> MUNCH
> So did it take you guys a long time to get pregnant?

VERONA

We don't know, actually. We weren't 100
percent trying . . . I mean, we wanted to
have a baby but this one . . . just came
ahead of schedule.

MUNCH

Oh. That's wonderful.

It's clear that Munch doesn't really find that news so wonderful.

MUNCH *(cont'd)*

Any problems so far?

VERONA

Not so far.
    (now sensing that she shouldn't be smug
        about this)
I've been crying a little more than usual.

MUNCH

Me too.

VERONA

You're not pregnant, are you?

MUNCH

No, no. No . . .

She seems about to say something but Tom and Burt—in high spirits—
burst over to the table.

TOM

We need real food. I need bacon.

MUNCH
(to Verona)
He eats a lot of bacon.

INT. REMO'S CAFE — MIDNIGHT

The four of them are in a booth. Tom is feasting on a large stack of pancakes, with an enormous side of bacon. The other three are drinking tea. Burt has a piece of apple pie.

TOM
(his face full of pig fat)
Wait. So you're still not married? Burt, when are you going to propose?

BURT
Propose? All I do is propose.
(to Verona)
Verona, will you marry me?

Verona does a quick shake of her head, as if she's saying no to fresh pepper on her salad.

MUNCH
(to Verona)
Is this true? It's you who's behind this?

VERONA
I can't see the point.

MUNCH
There isn't any, really. Not unless you have parents who care one way or the other,

which you don't. Maybe there isn't really a point. Is there a point, Tom?

Tom shrugs.

> MUNCH *(cont'd)*
> It's a nice tradition, though.

> BURT
> Your wedding was good. Really good.

> MUNCH
> It was, wasn't it?

Now Tom has finished his bacon and is ready to expound.

> TOM
> You know what you need to be happy, and sane and all that? You need this.

Tom is holding up the maple syrup.

> TOM *(cont'd)*
> Here's you two guys.

He takes two sugar cubes from the bowl on the table.

> TOM *(cont'd)*
> Or wait.

He replaces one of the sugars with a brown one.

> VERONA
> Thanks, Tom.

TOM

Okay. So you have you two. And let's say here's the baby.

He takes a smaller brown cube and adds it to the plate.

TOM *(cont'd)*

And here's your house.

He uses toothpicks to enclose the three of them in a very crude house, with a coaster for a roof.

TOM *(cont'd)*

But what is this? Is that home, is that a family? No, no. Course not. That's just the raw material—the people, the walls, the furniture, your jobs, maybe a grandmother.

VERONA

Glammie.

TOM

A glammie. So you've got the basics. But that's not a family, that's not a home. The thing that binds it all together is this.

Now he holds up the maple syrup.

BURT

Awesome.

He begins to pour it all over the sugar and toothpicks.

TOM

This is love.

BURT

I knew it.

TOM

This is your love, guys, your patience your
consideration, your better selves. Man, you
just have no idea how good you can be! But
you have to use all of it.
(the syrup is everywhere now, inches of it)
It's not like simple masonry, where you use
a little layer of mortar between each row of
bricks. With this, you have to use TONS of
it. For every brick, there's a half-ton of
mortar.

VERONA

I thought we were doing syrup.

TOM

Mortar, syrup—it's all the same. It's the
glue. It's all those good things you have in
you—the love, the wisdom, the generosity,
the selflessness, the patience. Patience at 3
a.m. when everyone's awake because
Ibrahim's sick and can't find the bathroom
and just puked in Katya's bed . . . And
patience when you blink and it's 5:30 and
it's time to get up again—and you know
you're going to be tired all day, all week,
all your life . . .

MUNCH

You're thinking, What happened to
Greece? To swimming naked off the coast
of Greece?

TOM

And you have to be willing to make the
family out of whatever you have. Why do
we have an Ethiopian boy, and girls from
Vietnam and the Black Sea? I don't know,
man!

MUNCH
(really showing her tipsiness now)
It makes no goddamned sense.

TOM

But then again, it does. It does! It's all
about sense. And stability. You know
James, the stray? He likes to eat dinner at 7
every night. That's what he wants! He
wants that predictability, right? So he
cooks for us sometimes—anything to
know that at 7, he'll be at a table, with five
other faces, a plate of hot food in front of
him.

MUNCH

You have to be so much better than you
ever thought.
(beat)
And once a week Tom and I go out and at
least one of us comes home wasted . . .
That's important.

TOM

Sometimes Munch gives me a hickey.
The kids are none the wiser.

MUNCH
(with a drunken wink)

Turtlenecks.

INT. CLUB — NIGHT — LATER

Burt and Tom are at a table near the stage, both of them drunk. There is a sign near the bar that reads AMATEUR BURLESQUE NIGHT. *Then below: Featuring the Music from the Sixties. The stage has red velvet curtains and a pole.*

Music is playing as four guys, amateurs and friends—or maybe co-workers in ties—are doing a clumsy, barely-choreographed dance with their shirts off.

BURT

This is new to me. It's like Dance Karaoke.

TOM

It's Montreal. World capital of this kind of
shit.

The guys finish up and stumble drunkenly off the stage.

BURT

This isn't gonna be all men, is it? Those
guys were really enjoyable but still—

TOM

Nah.

(suddenly not sure)

Hope not. Where's Rona?

BURT

Bathroom. Where's Munch?

Tom points to the stage onto which Munch is stepping. He's only semi-surprised.

The Beach Boys' "Don't Worry Baby" kicks in.

At first, Munch's dance is shy, innocent, cheerful. But she quickly gets more controlled, and the dance becomes darker and more intense.

She takes off her blouse, revealing a slinky tank-top.

BURT *(cont'd)*

Uh oh. She's got the pole. Don't you want
to say something?

TOM

Nah. Let her go.

Munch continues to dance—a desperate sort of routine, a dance of loss and defiance. The lyrics kick in:

Well it's been building up inside of me
for oh I don't know how long

Verona walks into the room at that moment. She sees Munch on the stage and freezes. After a moment, her eyes and Munch's meet; volumes pass between them.

153

TOM (*cont'd*)
(*to Burt, while still watching Munch*)
She had another miscarriage.

BURT

When?

The dance is getting wilder, more soulful.

TOM

Thursday.

BURT

No. Just this Thursday?—

TOM

Yeah.

Beat.

TOM (*cont'd*)
Hell, Burt. We've had too many of these.
The miscarriages, they take so much out of
you. This is her fifth. I know she loves all
those kids like they were her own blood,
but . . .

*They watch Munch. Verona hasn't moved—she's still standing, frozen.
The song is, in this context, powerful, searing, and Munch's dance is one of
great melancholy and raw power. At this point, Verona turns to Burt, and
they lock eyes. Tom continues talking to Burt, oblivious.*

TOM *(cont'd)*

I wonder if we've been selfish, people like
us. We wait until our thirties and then
we're surprised that the babies aren't so
easy to make anymore . . . And every day
another million fourteen-year-olds get
pregnant without trying . . . I just wish I
could make it work for her. If I could fix it
all and just make a baby for her. It's terrible
feeling this helpless, man. You just watch
these babies grow and then fade and you
don't know if you're supposed to name
them or bury them or . . . I'm sorry.

*The song is ending and Munch is stepping down from the stage to many
cheers.*

Tom helps Munch off the steps and she sits on his lap, holding him fiercely.

*From either side of the couple, Verona and Burt stare at each other
intensely, feeling very lucky, knowing too well the fragility of what they
have.*

INT. MONTREAL HOUSE — GUEST ROOM — NEXT MORNING

*Verona wakes up, hearing what seems to be a muffled conversation. She
looks over and sees that Burt's not there. She looks around; the voice she
hears is close, and is Burt's, but he's not visible. She looks in the bathroom,
the closets . . .*

BURT
(on phone)

You have every right to be pissed. Or worse.

(pause)

Damned right I'll be there. This afternoon. We'll leave as soon as Rone wakes up.

(beat)

No. Don't do that. You're always paying. Stop. I can swing it.

Eventually she squats down, realizing that Burt is—could he really be?—under the bed. He's on the phone. Finally he sees her.

BURT *(cont'd)*
(to the phone)

Hold on a sec. She's up.

(to Verona)

It's Courtney.

(back into the phone)

No. I'm telling her now.

(back to Verona)

We're going to Miami.

INT. MONTREAL HOUSE — GUEST ROOM — MORNING — LATER

Verona and Burt are getting dressed in a hurry.

VERONA
Why didn't he tell you sooner?

156

BURT

He's embarrassed.

VERONA

You're his brother.

BURT

But it's embarrassing if your wife leaves
you. She just left, Verona. They never
fought, nothing. She was— he knew what
I thought of her. I knew she always had one
eye open for something better.

VERONA

Poor Courtney. How old is Annabelle?

BURT

Eight.

VERONA

Jesus.

BURT

I know, I know.

They walk downstairs.

INT. MONTREAL HOUSE — LIVING ROOM — MORNING

*Munch and Tom, both wearing turtlenecks, look insanely awake and chip-
per for having stayed out late and woken so early. Munch is on her knees
fixing Katya's ponytail—she's getting ready for a soccer game; Cammie is*

*already in her soccer uniform and is coloring in, with a Sharpie, the parts
of her soccer ball that are worn out. Tom, with a big cup of coffee, is at the
jigsaw-puzzle table with Ibrahim. James is visible in the distance, in the
kitchen, eating his breakfast.*

> KATYA
>
> Man you guys can sleep!

> VERONA
> (to Munch and Tom)
>
> We've got to go.

> MUNCH
>
> What? Why?

> CAMMIE
>
> They're not wearing turtlenecks.

CUT TO:

INT. PLANE—DAY

*This time, the plane ride is more melancholy. They have a lot on their
minds. Verona sleeps across Burt's lap. All around them are soldiers—
National Guard of all ages—on their way to or from Iraq or elsewhere.*

Burt stares out of the window.

EXT. MIAMI—DAY

Burt's P.O.V. of Miami from the air.

INT. TAXI — MIAMI — LATE AFTERNOON

Burt and Verona ride, still preoccupied by the news of Courtney's wife's departure. The stunning scenery has no effect on them.

EXT. COURTNEY'S OFFICE — LATE AFTERNOON

They arrive at Burt's brother's office. It's in a small house just outside of Miami's downtown. The skyline is visible in the background. It's a cozy dentist's office with signs out front that welcome kids.

INT. COURTNEY'S DENTAL OFFICE — LATE AFTERNOON

It's cozy inside too, though the waiting room is decorated with posters and memorabilia celebrating the supremacy of the 1970s tennis star Björn Borg.

Sitting at the appointment window is not an adult secretary but a girl of eight. She has a pencil behind her ear. This is ANNABELLE.

She hears the bells when the door opens, but doesn't look up.

> ANNABELLE
> Are you Mrs. Alvarez?

> VERONA
> No. Are you . . . eight?

Annabelle looks up and brightens when she sees Verona. Burt emerges from behind Verona and Annabelle's face explodes into a phosphorescent smile.

ANNABELLE

Burp!

BURT

Hey Bellbottom! Come here.

Burt's niece is cute in an awkward sort of way, with dark rings around her eyes. Seeing Burt has her face contorted into a wild sort of grin.

She can't wait—she crawls through the window and jumps off the edge and into Burt's arms. Burt lifts her over his head and then hugs her for a long moment.

BURT *(cont'd)*
(whispering into her hair)

Hi sweetie-pie poop-a-loop. I missed you
so much.

Annabelle is too deep in a bliss-high to speak. She rests her chin on Burt's neck and chews her gum silently, her tiny finger playing in Burt's hair.

The moment is broken by a loud yelp from inside.

PATIENT (O.S.)

Holy mother of God!

In a few seconds, COURTNEY, *about 37, with shaggy hair and glasses, emerges. There's blood on his uniform.*

COURTNEY
(wiping his hands)

Hey! I thought you weren't coming till
tonight.

160

                              BURT
We got an early flight.

                            COURTNEY
Verona! You look fantastic.

*He gives her a warm hug. While they embrace, he sees Burt and almost
instantly tears up.*

He and Burt hug.

                        COURTNEY *(cont'd)*
Hey brother.

                              BURT
Hey man.
                    (pulling out of the embrace)
Can you leave now?

                            COURTNEY
Yeah. Maria?

Maria, a young dental assistant, walks in.

                              MARIA
Yes?

                            COURTNEY
Can you finish Mr. Hyland?

                              MARIA
I don't—

> COURTNEY

Do your best.

EXT. COURTNEY'S OFFICE/MIAMI STREET — LATE AFTERNOON

They leave the office and walk out to the street. Courtney looks up at the sun as if he hasn't seen it in weeks.

> COURTNEY

I'll drive. You hungry? I'm here.

They arrive at his car. It's a new Volvo.

> BURT

Nice.

Courtney can't find his keys.

> COURTNEY

I had 'em here.

He looks in his backpack. No luck. He checks and rechecks his pockets.

> COURTNEY *(cont'd)*

Belle, did I give em to you?

> ANNABELLE

No.

Now he's looking under the car.

BURT

You think they're under the car?

COURTNEY

Shush! I have a spare down here.
(*fumbling under the car*)
GODDAMMIT.

He gets up, and slowly composes himself.

COURTNEY (*cont'd*)
(*adopting a tone somewhere between saccharine and about-to-explode*)
Bella, are you sure I didn't give them to you? Remember that sometimes you're wrong. You were wrong yesterday when I asked if you had already brought in the mail and then we didn't see that check that Dad needed. Remember that?

Annabelle nods.

COURTNEY (*cont'd*)
So do you have them?

ANNABELLE

No.

COURTNEY
(*very loud*)

Ahhhhhh!

They all stand for a beat, not quite knowing what to do, surprised at Courtney's outburst.

Seeing all four of them standing by the corner, a cab slows, and Burt hails it.

BURT

> Get in.

Verona and Annabelle get in.

Courtney goes to get in. Burt stops him.

BURT *(cont'd)*

> Hey. This isn't you. You need a second? Want to run around the block or something?

Courtney softens a bit.

COURTNEY
(still tense)

> I'm okay. Sorry. Sorry.

They get in.

EXT. WATERFRONT — NIGHT — LATER

They're all walking along the South Beach promenade.

Verona and Annabelle walk ahead, inexplicably giving military salutes to everyone they pass. They pass a parent with a five-year-old boy on a leash. Annabelle and Verona exchange looks.

Burt and Courtney walk a ways behind. Courtney's still very tense.

                    BURT
Have you heard from her?

                  COURTNEY
Not a word.

They walk a few steps.

                COURTNEY *(cont'd)*
You didn't see this coming, did you? She
was normal, right?

                    BURT
Sure.

                  COURTNEY
You didn't tell Mom and Dad, did you?

Burt shakes his head.

                COURTNEY *(cont'd)*
I will eventually. I just . . . They never
liked her anyway.

They walk.

                COURTNEY *(cont'd)*
You know how many times I've checked our
messages? It's a tic now. Ten times an hour. I
got all the lines to bounce to my cell.
                    (beat)
I have to invent new ways of dealing with
it every night. I can't sleep. I destroyed all
the lawn furniture with a golf club.

                    165

Burt sees a chance to ease the tension.

> BURT

Wedge?

Courtney laughs a little.

> COURTNEY

Driver. Ruined it.

Courtney softens.

> COURTNEY *(cont'd)*

Part of me is so angry I never want to hear her name again. But if she came back tomorrow and said she was sorry I'd be so fucking relieved. The weight! I feel like a meteor hit me.

> BURT

Belle seems okay.

> COURTNEY

Yeah. That's even weirder.

> BURT

What'd you tell her?

> COURTNEY

At first I said it was a business trip. I made the mistake of telling her it'd be five days. I actually thought that was a conservative estimate. I thought I'd have figured it out by then. Then five days went by and Belle

wanted to know where she was. So I said
her grandpa died.

BURT

You told her Dad died?

COURTNEY

No, Helena's dad. It took her mind off of
her mom for a while.

They walk.

COURTNEY *(cont'd)*

Burt, I really need help. With what to do
next. Sorry I called. I just . . . My head's
getting cloudy. If she's really gone for
good, I need to know what to say. It's
wrong to tell Belle she was murdered,
right?

BURT

That might be traumatic.

COURTNEY

Yeah, but there's finality there . . .

They enter a restaurant.

INT. COURTNEY'S HOUSE — LATER THAT
NIGHT

*Courtney, Burt and Verona are all sitting on Annabelle's bed, acting out a
story together.*

COURTNEY

And then the bullfrog said . . .

Silence. All eyes are on Verona.

VERONA

Wait, was that me? I'm the bullfrog, too?

The answer is yes. Verona looks at the page.

VERONA *(cont'd)*
(adopting the voice of a bullfrog)
Where is my crown? I need my crown!

COURTNEY

And to that the wolverine said:

BURT
(in a German accent)
"You vill nevah have your crown, stinky
bullfrog! I have buried it under zah giant
boabab tree! Ha ha ha ha ha!"

Burt's wolverine voice and maniacal laugh are a bit over the top.

COURTNEY

And so the story ends. At least tonight it
does. Say goodnight to Uncle Burp and
Verona.

*Burt and Verona each lean down and give hugs to Annabelle, who seems
desperately happy that they're there.*

Annabelle settles into bed. Courtney and Burt leave. Annabelle looks at Verona.

> ANNABELLE
> Will you stay a little longer?

Courtney hears this and nods that it's okay.

> VERONA
> Of course I will, Bellie.

She sits down on Annabelle's bed. Annabelle seems greatly relieved that she doesn't have to say goodbye just yet.

INT. COURTNEY'S KITCHEN — SIMULTANEOUS

Burt and Courtney are in the kitchen. Courtney's just opened beers for them, and they clink them together. From the kitchen, they can see Verona in Annabelle's room, singing quietly to her.

On the kitchen table, there are various papers—bills, forms, notices from school. Courtney's clearly overwhelmed.

In the mess, Courtney finds something.

> COURTNEY
> You see this?

It's Annabelle's new school picture.

> BURT
> (examining it)
> Man, she is so cute.

169

COURTNEY

She just took this on Monday. Remember
when we had to wait weeks for the school
pictures?

BURT

Yeah . . .
               (*noticing something*)
What's on her upper lip?

COURTNEY

Carrot juice.

BURT

Huh.

COURTNEY

I didn't see it. I don't see the carrot juice on
her mouth when she leaves the house. I'm
never going to see these things. Moms see
the carrot juice on their daughters'
mouths. Moms know when their daughters
aren't dressed right. Moms go shopping
with them, and make sure their hair
doesn't look spazzy. In one fell swoop
Helena has changed this girl's life from a
normal one, where she can be popular and
all that, to the distinct likelihood that she's
going to be introverted, a poor dresser—
one of those kids who looks all longingly at
the girls who have new shoes and the right
backpack . . .

BURT

At least it was carrot juice. Not whisky or . . . glue.

COURTNEY

It's just the beginning, though. Things devolve from here. I'll be spending every waking moment trying to reconstruct a normal life, but Annabelle will always be the girl without a mom.

They both look to Annabelle's room, where Verona continues to sing gently to her while slowly stroking her hair.

INT. COURTNEY'S HOUSE, BATHROOM— NIGHT—MUCH LATER

Verona is brushing her teeth, and realizes she doesn't know where Burt is.

INT. COURTNEY'S HOUSE, GUEST BEDROOM— NIGHT

She looks for him first in the bedroom.

INT. COURTNEY'S HOUSE, KITCHEN—NIGHT

Then she looks in the kitchen, and finally hears his muffled voice. Through the sliding door Verona sees Burt on the back patio, with a phonebook open, pacing while talking on his cellphone.

BURT

Who am I? Who are you? Well, I know who you are. What? I think you know more than you're letting on. Hello? Hello!?

EXT. COURTNEY'S PATIO/BACKYARD — NIGHT

Verona comes outside and joins him.

VERONA

What are you doing?

BURT

I'm calling anyone she knew. Her old company, her friends—

VERONA

At midnight.

BURT

Right! Element of surprise.

Verona notices the broken patio furniture—victims of Courtney's frustration.

VERONA

Stop, please.

Burt sits down. Then stands up. He's so agitated he can't stay still. Finally he gets onto Annabelle's trampoline—a big rectangular one, three feet off the ground.

BURT
(now jumping)
What kind of Goddamned person would
leave her daughter?

VERONA
(watching him go up and down)
I don't know. Maybe not such a strong person. Please stop.

BURT
(not stopping)
And there's nothing we can do. She's gone.
This family can't be fixed. That's it. What
if one of us freaks out like that?

VERONA
We won't. And it can be fixed and you
know it. And if you don't stop jumping I
will find a way to hurt you with that shovel.

She points to a large iron shovel. Burt stops jumping.

VERONA *(cont'd)*
C'mere. Sit down.

*She pulls him down onto the trampoline. Soon they're both on their knees,
on the trampoline, facing each other.*

BURT
But really—what if something happens to
one of us and makes us crazy? Like what if I
walk by a construction site and something
falls and my frontal lobe gets chopped off

and my personality is altered and then I'm
not a good dad. What if that happens?

Verona doesn't know how much she should humor him.

                    VERONA
We'll be careful walking near construction
sites.

                     BURT
And what about Munch?

                    VERONA
She'll be careful near construction sites,
too.

                     BURT
No, really. Don't you just look at her and
want to give her everything she wants? It's
so unfair—

                    VERONA
Of course it's unfair. She can't have a baby,
and bad parents still get to be parents, and
good parents die when their daughters are
in high school. So what.

                     BURT
I'm sorry, Rone.

                    VERONA
All we can do is be good for this one baby.
We don't have control over much else.

BURT

Let's get married at least.

VERONA

Never.

Burt's visibly disappointed. He really thought she'd say yes this time.

VERONA *(cont'd)*

But I'll never leave you.

BURT
(dejected)

Yeah.

VERONA

I promise.

BURT

Okay.
(pause)
You promise to never marry me because you
don't want to marry me without your parents there—and I get that—and you promise to never leave me. But do you promise to
never leave this baby we're having?

VERONA

I do. And do you promise to stop talking
about your ability to find or not find my
vagina after I give birth?

BURT

I do. And do you promise to let me cobble—

VERONA

Carve.

BURT

To carve in my spare time and teach our daughter the lure of the great Mississippi?

VERONA

I do. And do you promise that when she talks you'll listen—like really listen—especially when she's scared? And that her fights will be your fights?

They're lying down now, face-to-face.

BURT

I do. And do you promise to let our daughter be fat or skinny or any weight at all because we want her to be happy no matter what and eating disorders are too cliché for our daughter?

VERONA

I do. And do you never to develop a thing for seahorses?

BURT
(laughing)

I do. And do you promise, if I die in some embarrassing or mundane way, that you'll lie and tell our daughter that her father was killed by Russian soldiers in intense hand-to-hand combat so he could save 850 Chechen orphans?

They're both fading now. Verona's eyes are closed.

> VERONA
> Yes, Chechen orphans . . . I do . . .
> I do.

They are asleep.

EXT. COURTNEY'S BACKYARD —
TRAMPOLINE — DAWN

*Burt and Verona are entwined on the trampoline, a tarpaulin is pulled
over them.*

*Dawn is breaking. Verona opens her eyes. In the yard there is an orange
tree with some new, young oranges on it.*

Burt moans himself awake.

> VERONA
> We had an orange tree.

> BURT
> Who?

> VERONA
> When we were kids.

*Burt pricks up his ears; Verona so rarely speaks about her childhood. For a
change, he knows to be quiet.*

VERONA *(cont'd)*

My dad was really proud of it. He planted
it one spring and he kept going out there
first thing every morning to see if any
oranges had grown. But nothing ever grew.
The thing was sickly or something or the
soil wasn't right. So one morning, my mom
woke Grace and me up at like 5 o'clock.
We had to be super quiet. She led us outside to the tree with two grocery bags filled
with oranges—and pineapples and grapes
and melons for some reason. We hung the
fruit from the tree using string and
tape . . . It actually worked. Then we all
slouched down in the front seat of the
truck waiting for my dad to come out . . .

BURT

What'd he say?

VERONA

Well, he stared at the tree for a full minute,
just stared at it. I think he first thought
they were real. That the tree had burst into
fruit overnight. Then he saw the pineapples, I guess, and he started laughing
harder than we'd ever heard him laugh.
Grace and I ran out of the truck squealing.
My mom followed. From then on, every
once in a while, one of us would hang fruit
there. Usually something plastic . . . Pears,
strawberries, bananas . . .

Verona and Burt look at each other. They're both thinking the same thing.

Annabelle calls from the doorway.

> ANNABELLE
> You're supposed to come inside like nor-
> mal people and eat food that normal people
> eat. Inside like normal people.
> > *(beat)*
> Are you normal or not?

They go inside.

INT. COURTNEY'S HOUSE — MORNING

They're all eating breakfast. We catch them mid-conversation. Burt and Verona have figured out where they're going next—where they're probably going to live—and have just told Courtney. .

> BURT
> You're welcome to come. There's room.

> COURTNEY
> It sounds great. I think it's the right thing
> for you guys. But no, I've decided I want to
> stay here for now. I'll figure it out . . . sorry
> about yesterday.

From off camera two girls' voices:

> VOICES (O.S.)
> Belle! Belle!

They look to the front door where, behind the screen, we see two kids, who are all dressed and headed to school together. They're waiting for Annabelle.

COURTNEY
(to Belle, who's shoveling her oatmeal into her mouth)
Hurry up.
(to Burt and Verona)
She's in the school play. She's the lead.

VERONA
(to Annabelle)
Really? What's the play?

ANNABELLE
(with a mouth full, using her spoon to make a stabbing motion)
Medea.

Annabelle gives hugs to Burt and Verona and leaves with her friends. They all watch. Courtney is smiling. Annabelle calls from outside.

ANNABELLE (O.S.) *(cont'd)*
Bye!

COURTNEY
We'll definitely visit when the baby's born.
Is, uh, Grace coming?
(he shares a lewd look with Burt)

VERONA
Ew.

COURTNEY
Hey—I was just asking. Idle curiosity.

INT. BURT AND VERONA'S CAR — SOUTH CAROLINA — DAY

It's late spring.

We see a blue Volvo with luggage tied to the top.

Burt and Verona (now more pregnant) are driving through an unfamiliar landscape. It's hilly, semirural, beautiful, maybe a bit run-down.

> BURT
>
> Is it starting to look familiar?

> VERONA
> *(uncertain)*
>
> I think so . . . I want it to . . . But I also want it to be new, you know? New for us? New enough to feel like we found it. Does that make sense?

> BURT
>
> It does.

> VERONA
>
> Turn here. *(now more nervous)* I think this is it . . .

They head down a narrow winding road canopied by wisteria and kudzu. Burt is clearly in heaven; it's the landscape of his dreams.

Suddenly Verona takes in a quick breath. Burt sees what she's seeing: the tree. It's older and not in such great shape. Two or three old pieces of plastic fruit still hang from it. Verona stares, her eyes welling. They say nothing.

EXT. BEAUTIFUL SEMIRURAL CUL-DE-SAC, SOUTH CAROLINA — DAY

They pull up to a Victorian house, three-storied and grand, though in disrepair. Burt brings the car to a stop.

> BURT
>
> You ready?

> VERONA
>
> I am. Are you?

> BURT
>
> I am.

They get out of the car.

> VERONA
>
> I forgot how beautiful . . .

We realize this is Verona's childhood home, the same house we saw in the photo in Grace and Verona's offices. It's dilapidated but full of character and potential.

There's a creek running through the property; a bridge over it connects the driveway to the front door. Burt is astounded, taking it all in.

> BURT
>
> I love your parents so much right now. They were geniuses.

As they walk toward the front door, Verona leans on Burt for strength. She hasn't been back home in ten years.

INT. VICTORIAN HOUSE, SOUTH CAROLINA—
  DAY

They enter the house. It's very dark. Burt opens the dusty curtains and light suddenly streams in revealing wood floors, a beautiful stairway, with a banister. Verona looks up the stairs.

Burt enters the living room. He stands in the center of the room, looking around.

Burt comes into the entrance hall to discover Verona sitting on the bottom stair. A few tears are running down her face. He sits next to her on the bottom step and puts his arm around her.

> BURT
> This is really us, don't you think?

> VERONA
> I hope so.

Verona wipes her tears away and turns to look at Burt. She smiles.

> VERONA *(cont'd)*
> I really fucking hope so.

We pull back until we're outside the door.

The door closes.

THE END.

NOTE TO READER

What follows is the original ending to the movie, as it was written in early 2006. We thought we'd include it, as evidence of the way the movie was originally conceived. This was of course a very dark time in American history. The war in Iraq was at a low point, and the administration of George W. Bush was sowing fear and paranoia at every level. While finishing the script, we brought our two-month-old daughter on a short trip, and at the airports we passed through, our infant was repeatedly subjected to searches, wherein we had to undress her so security people could actually pat her down. It was madness, and emblematic of how much we'd all lost perspective. So the ending that follows seemed to be the only rational choice for a couple bringing a baby into the world.

By the time the movie was being filmed and released, things had changed significantly in the country, and we felt this ending was no longer as appropriate.

To set this up: In the following scenes, Burt and Verona are still in Miami visiting with Courtney and Annabelle. Their long-time friends Ron and Sue are having a bris—a Jewish ceremony wherein a newborn is circumcised amid family and friends. They all attend the bris together.

EXT. ROB AND SUE'S HOUSE — MIDMORNING

Burt, Verona, Courtney and Annabelle—holding Verona's hand—are outside the door. Courtney rings the bell.

> VERONA
>
> Ron and Sue . . . Are they still doing . . .
> web . . . things?

Burt nods. The door opens. It's RON *and* SUE. *Ron and Sue are the parents of the bris boy. They're sane and good-humored.*

> SUE
> *(to Verona)*
> You look great!

They all embrace. Verona and Annabelle follow Sue into a side bedroom.

> RON
>
> I didn't know your parents were moving to
> Belgium.

> BURT
>
> Yeah.
> *(now looking around)*
> I didn't know you were Jewish. Or were
> gonna be Jewish.

> RON
>
> That's why we had the hoopah at the wed-
> ding, Burt. The . . .

(gesturing the shape of a hoopah with his hands)

BURT

Oh I liked that thing!

Sue and Verona join them.

SUE

Tough luck with the grandparents moving
to Belgium. It's not Antwerp, is it?

*All six survey the throng of guests. Everyone's drinking bad red wine,
which has stained everyone's lips and teeth.*

RON
(genuinely curious)
We don't know these people.

SUE

But they're all gonna see our son's penis
mutilated.

RON

I think there's a circuit—people who come
to all the brises. Like garage-sale people.
(to Burt)
You want some olives? Everything else
seems to involve hummus.

BURT

You're offering me an olive?

Ron is half-heartedly holding a small bowl of olives.

RON

I have no idea.

Ron slowly puts the down the bowl of olives, carefully, having regained his senses, as if setting down a loaded gun. Their attention turns to a TV, where images of Iraq play. The commentator: "Experts now estimate that American soldiers will be in Iraq for at least five more years, and the casualties are likely to enter the 5,000-dead range . . . "

Verona is standing alone, near the kitchen. From behind her she hears voices.

> OLD WOMAN'S VOICE
> It's a girl.

> ANOTHER OLD WOMAN
> How can you tell?

> FIRST OLD WOMAN
> That's when you gain weight everywhere.

Verona realizes they're talking about her. She turns to find two very old women, neither over five feet tall.

> VERONA
> Are you really saying this to me?

> FIRST OLD WOMAN
> I've never been wrong.

> VERONA
> Well, as a matter of fact, it is a girl.

> SECOND OLD WOMAN
> You found out? No.

FIRST OLD WOMAN

Why would you want to find out? The
miracle of birth! It's the great surprise of
life!

SECOND OLD WOMAN
*(not-so-quietly whispering to the first old
woman)*

Instant gratification. Even with the babies.
That's where the cloning comes from.

They take a moment to look pityingly on Verona.

FIRST OLD WOMAN

Ooh! Olives!

RABBI (O.S.)

It is time!

*The party moves over to the living room, where the rabbi has unveiled his
tools on the dining room table and is ready to begin. Sue brings the baby
over.*

RON

You want to be part of it?

COURTNEY

No.

BURT
(emphatically)

Yes.

All right. I'm gonna hold the feet. You
take this . . .
  (*handing him a small cloth dipped in wine*)
. . . and give it to him when he's crying.
It'll take the edge off.

BURT

Awesome.

Burt puffs up proudly with the responsibility.

*The rabbi chants and the audience gathers around. Verona is in the next
room, avoiding the crowd.*

*The bris baby is wailing. Burt can be seen frantically applying more wine
to the cloth, to no avail. The baby screams until the rabbi takes charge. He
grabs the infant and swings him up and down in an incredibly fast
motion—making huge Us in the air. The baby is immediately calm.*

Burt approaches Verona at the back of the room.

BURT (*cont'd*)
  (*holding up his purple index finger*)
Look, I voted.

He gets no reaction.

BURT (*cont'd*)
Did you see me?

VERONA

Sort of.

CUT TO:

INT. RON AND SUE'S KITCHEN

TIPSY GUY

Annabelle!

He crouches down in front of her. He needs to put his fingers on the ground, football-style, to steady himself.

TIPSY GUY (cont'd)

You remember me?

His teeth are stained purple.

TIPSY GUY (cont'd)

Sure you do. You tease. Listen. I wanna say something. I'm gonna get a little heavy on you. Thing is, Annabelle, is that I don't want you to feel responsible for this. I've known your mom for a long time—I knew her back in high school when she played tennis. And the thing you should know is that she was always a flake. Okay? I don't even know WHY I remember this, but she stood ME up one time. This was formal— senior year. A big deal. I had rented a DeLorean—you know what that is?

Annabelle shakes her head.

>   TIPSY GUY *(cont'd)*
>   *(demonstrating)*
> It's a car with gull-wing doors and this
> awesome . . .

Annabelle turns and walks away.

>   TIPSY GUY *(cont'd)*
> Hey. Hey kid. Don't walk away from me.
> Hey, flake-like-your-mom kid!

Annabelle continues out the back door and into the yard. She finds a small bench and lays on it, stomach down.

CUT TO:

INT. HALLWAY — BRIS HOME

Burt and Verona are talking to a clean-cut WASPy type in a suit.

>   MAN
> I honestly don't care about the wiretap-
> ping. Whatever it takes. And it's not like
> they're listening in to MY conversation,
> right? They know what they're doing.
> They know where to draw the line . . .

Courtney approaches.

>   COURTNEY
> You guys seen Belle?

VERONA

No.

COURTNEY

I'm sure she's around here . . .

Courtney wanders off.

MAN

If they wanna strip-search me at church it's
fine with me. They keep us safe, we keep
our mouths shut . . .

*Now Burt and Verona are preoccupied, looking for Annabelle. Burt
catches sight of Courtney heading into the back yard.*

VERONA

We should help.

BURT

Excuse us . . .

Burt and Verona head into the backyard, too.

CUT TO:

EXT. BACKYARD — SLIGHTLY LATER

*Verona, Burt, Courtney, Annabelle, Rob, Sue, and their baby all sit out-
side on the lawn furniture and on the grass. They're depleted by all the
activity inside. In the house, it's all bustle and gossip—the brightly lit
house is jammed and very loud. They watch it as if it were a house on fire
and they've just escaped.*

193

BURT

You know what it looked like? A cigar cut-
ter. Like they just snip so quickly . . .
> (demonstrating)

. . . those two blades meeting around
the . . .

COURTNEY

Ahem.

Annabelle is upset, clinging to Courtney, and won't look back at the house.

COURTNEY *(cont'd)*

Feels good to get out of there.
> (to Sue and Ron)

No offense.

SUE

None taken.

RON
> (to Burt and Verona)

So where to next, guys? Are you on some
kind of vacation or? . . .

COURTNEY

They're looking for a place to live. They
can live anywhere.

VERONA

You can, too, Court. Anywhere people have
teeth.
> (to Sue and Ron)

We all could.

SUE

Huh.

RON

We were actually thinking of leaving the country.

SUE

We used to at least. After 2000, we thought about it, then we forgot about it, now we're thinking about it again.

RON

Vaguely at least. I want to go somewhere that doesn't have an army. Isn't there some-place that doesn't have an army?

VERONA

What, like Germany?

RON

No, no. There are other places. I mean, wouldn't that sort of be a statement right there, to pack up and . . . Anyway.

This is very interesting to Burt and Verona.

INT. RESTAURANT — NEXT MORNING

They're all there—Burt, Verona, Sue, Ron, their baby, Courtney, and Annabelle. The conversation is continuing as if it never stopped.

VERONA

But are we copping out?

BURT

We're waiting till things get sane again. It'll happen. We can just sit it out for a while.

COURTNEY

I don't know. It's a crazy idea.
(beat)
And I like crazy, usually. But right now I'm not such a fan of crazy.

RON

But just to be free of the tension, the paranoia. Just think . . .

BURT

And we can always come back.

They all contemplate this. Courtney seems skeptical.

INT. CAR — ALL OF THEM IN ONE MINIVAN

The conversation continues . . .

VERONA

It's sort of like dropping out, I guess. But we'll have a phone. Will we have a phone?

2 Dec 02 Hachette Book Group $62 108807

They turn off the road and down a dirt path, and into a compound—a clearing with five houses on it, each overlooking the water. The Costa Rican flag flies overhead.

They all step out of the car.

VERONA

I hope this isn't the dumbest idea ever.

ANNABELLE

(running by)

I don't think it is. I was getting sick of that place.

THE END.

SUE

I asked about that. The place has a phone.
It actually has a satellite dish, but I'm for
junking it.

BURT

What do you all think of a boat? Any of
you know how to sail?

No one knows how to sail.

BURT *(cont'd)*
The open seas . . .

INT. AIRPORT — DAY — A WEEK LATER

*Except for Courtney and Annabelle, they're all at the airport—Burt,
Verona, Sue, Ron, and their baby. They're in the security line, and Sue
and Ron's baby is being patted down by a security guard, under a gigantic
American flag and a sign that says* YOUR SECURITY IS OUR OBSESSION.
*Meanwhile, Verona's stomach is being wanded. It's all utterly horrifying
but our group is strangely cheerful.*

BURT
*(to Verona, as they're leaving the security
checkpoint)*
Never seen you so mellow about that.

VERONA

It won't happen again for a long time.

Burt's phone rings.

BURT
(*on phone, in his real voice*)
You're coming? You are? I can't believe it.
I'm . . . That's so good. We'll wait here.

He hangs up.

BURT (*cont'd*)
(*to everyone, tears in his eyes*)
They're coming.
    They all cheer.

INT. DIFFERENT MINIVAN, DRIVING
THROUGH A LUSH COUNTRYSIDE

Everyone's here: Burt, Verona, Courtney, Annabelle, Ron and Sue and their baby. They're all elated, taking in the scenery. They come around a bend and suddenly the ocean is visible—the sun is above, casting a wide glorious shimmer across the Pacific.

VERONA
Wow, this is strange.

COURTNEY
Strange that we can do this.

BURT
Anyone can do this.